A DORLING KINDERSLEY BOOK
www.dk.com

Chronicle 98
Written, edited, and designed by
GLS Editorial and Design
Garden Studios, 11-15 Betterton Street
London WC2H 9HP

GLS EDITORIAL AND DESIGN

Project editor Sasha Heseltine
Design director Ruth Shane
Editorial director Reg Grant

Written by Reg Grant

Contributors Adrian Gilbert, Victoria Sorzano

Picture researcher Will Hoon and Jo Walton
Indexer Kay Ollerenshaw

DORLING KINDERSLEY

Managing editor Frank Ritter
Managing art editor Derek Coombs
Production manager Ian Paton
Publisher Mike Edwards

PUBLISHER'S NOTE

Chronicle 98 covers events of the period mid-November 1997 to mid-November 1998 – a full 12 months of news. Readers of *Chronicle 97*, last year's edition, will have noted our move away from presenting the news of a strict calendar year. This change has been made to expand the market for the book and thereby safeguard the future of the series. We hope you enjoy *Chronicle 98* and we look forward to publishing *Chronicle 99*, our special end-of-millennium edition.

First published in Great Britain in 1998
by Dorling Kindersley Limited
9 Henrietta Street, London WC2E 8PS

A CIP catalogue record for this book is available from the British Library
ISBN 0 7513 0656 8

Reproduced by Goodfellow & Egan, Peterborough
Printed and bound in Italy by L.E.G.O.

Chronicle 98

A year of news as it happened

Mid-November 1997 to mid-November 1998

DORLING KINDERSLEY

LONDON • NEW YORK • SYDNEY • MOSCOW
www.dk.com

Peace and youth offer hope in year of scandals

Schooldays begin: Prince Harry joins his elder brother William at Eton College.

Many of the headlines of 1998 made depressing reading. Terrorism once more left its mark, with the town of Omagh suffering a terrible outrage at the hands of the bombers. In the United States, President Bill Clinton underwent public humiliation when confronted with salacious details of White House sexual encounters. Yet 1998 was also a year of hope. The Good Friday agreement created a real possibility of peace in Northern Ireland after 30 years of conflict. And young people of promise held out the prospect of a brighter future.

Young hopeful: England's 18-year-old striker Michael Owen celebrates a World Cup goal against Romania.

> "They hope that their mother and her memory will now finally be allowed to rest in peace."
>
> Statement issued on behalf of Prince William and Prince Harry, September 3, 1998.

In years to come, 1998 may well be remembered most for the emergence on to the public stage of a new generation with fresh attitudes.

The young royal princes, William and Harry, won many hearts with their courage in overcoming the tragic death of their mother. Their natural charm enchanted the public and seemed set to repair much of the damage done to the monarchy by the scandals of recent times.

Football's World Cup finals, which obsessed most of the nation in mid-summer, were also a triumph for youth, bringing England striker Michael Owen to prominence at the age of 18 – hailed by some of the world's sporting press as a new Pele.

The year's biggest political story in Britain was the drive for peace in Ulster. Northern Ireland Secretary Mo Mowlam made herself the most popular politician in Britain with her bluff, no nonsense style, but it was Northern Ireland politicians David Trimble and John Hume who won the Nobel Peace Prize.

Britain had its own pale reflection of the Clinton sex scandal in the Ron Davies affair. But as Clinton's popularity soared in America, there seemed good reason to hope that the public, while still fascinated by prurient stories, had stopped judging politicians by their private lives.

Teen idol: 16-year-old Prince William is mobbed by young admirers in Canada.

Co-winner of the Nobel Peace Prize: First Minister of Northern Ireland, David Trimble.

"They have voted to take the gun out of politics."

Northern Ireland Secretary Mo Mowlam, on the referendum vote in favour of the Good Friday peace accord, May 23, 1998.

Northern Ireland peacemaker: Mo Mowlam proved the right person to draw all sides into the peace process.

Terrorist outrage: The aftermath of the bomb explosion in Omagh in which 28 people were killed and more than 200 injured.

Presidential pursuer: Paula Jones alleged that Clinton sexually harassed her.

Reluctant witness: Monica Lewinsky gave evidence against Clinton to avoid prosecution.

Owning up: President Clinton admits at last that he had an "inappropriate relationship" with Monica Lewinsky.

"I did not have sexual relations with that woman."

President Bill Clinton on Monica Lewinsky, January 26, 1998.

Marriage under pressure: Hillary Clinton stood by her man despite his infidelity.

Triumphs and heartache in World Cup year

Indomitable champion: Prince Naseem Hamed celebrates another successful defence of his world featherweight title.

The 1998 sporting year was inevitably dominated by the football World Cup finals in France. The English and Scottish fans experienced a rollercoaster of emotions before both British teams went out with heads held high. Elsewhere, there was more for British sports lovers to cheer. The British athletics team scored a notable triumph in the European championships; three British drivers, David Coulthard, Eddie Irvine, and Damon Hill, figured in the top six in the Formula One drivers' championship; and England's cricketers won a Test series at last, beating South Africa.

Crashing out: Alexander Wurz of Benetton catapults over Jean Alesi in the Canadian Grand Prix, one of several spectacular crashes in this year's Formula One season.

"We are on the verge of something special."

British athletics executive David Moorcroft, after British athletes won nine gold medals in the European championships, August 23, 1998.

Apart from the British interest, the World Cup finals saw some attractive football, but top sides such as Brazil failed to show the quality expected of them, and referees were goaded by the authorities into a destructive blitz of red cards. In club football, it was Arsenal's year. The north London side won the Premiership and FA Cup double, a feat they previously achieved in 1971.

In tennis, Tim Henman rescued his career from apparent decline to reach the Wimbledon semi-finals and take over as British No. 1 from Greg Rusedski. In golf, Mark O'Meara astonished everyone by winning two major tournaments in a season after a long career in which he had won none. And young British amateur Justin Rose performed well enough to suggest a glorious future lay ahead.

Golden sprinter: Darren Campbell, 100m winner in the European championships in Budapest.

Passing the Test: England's cricketers celebrate winning the summer's Test series against South Africa.

"He is going to regret it for a long, long time."

Former England manager Bobby Robson on the foul that saw David Beckham sent off in the World Cup match against Argentina, June 30, 1998.

Hero to villain: David Beckham scores a spectacular goal against Colombia; he was then sent off in England's next World Cup match against Argentina.

Controversial leader: England football manager Glenn Hoddle.

"We could have gone all the way and won it."

England manager Glenn Hoddle on the World Cup, after his team's defeat by Argentina, July 1, 1998.

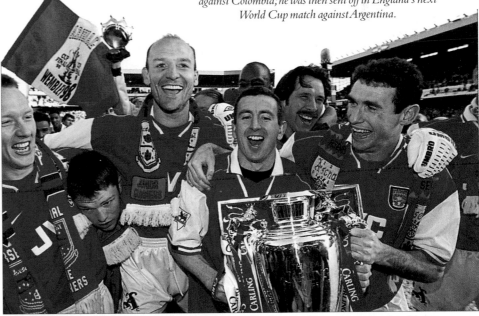

Double joy: The Arsenal team celebrate winning the FA Carling Premiership trophy, the first leg of their cup and league double in the 1997-98 season. Arsenal had achieved the double once before, in 1970-71.

Painted fans: The supporters were often among the stars of the World Cup – here from Nigeria (above) and Scotland (right).

Budding talent: British amateur Justin Rose, 17, takes the Open at Royal Birkdale by storm.

Studs, bumps, heart-throbs, and beauties

This year was notable for women's bold determination to be proud of their bodies and show them off in whatever state they might be. Melanie Blatt of girl-group All Saints set a fashion for revealing pregnancy bumps. The craze for body-piercing that has been gathering ground for some years reached the point at which a member of the Royal Family, Zara Phillips, could happily appear with a tongue stud. There were also some startlingly revealing dresses in use – for example, by Emma Noble, the fiancée of former prime minister John Major's son James. Bodies were definitely in.

There was no doubt, however, that men could be sex objects as well. Leonardo DiCaprio, angel-faced star of *Titanic*, was swooned over by millions of young women. The other films of the year included the much-praised *Good Will Hunting*, the bizarre *The Truman Show*, and the British gangster movie *Lock, Stock and Two Smoking Barrels*, which broke box-office records in its first week.

New faces on the celebrity pages included Denise van Outen, the presenter who enlivened Channel 4's *The Big Breakfast*, and teen sensation Billie Piper from Swindon, who powered her way into the pop charts.

Celebrity smiles: *Big Breakfast* presenter Denise van Outen with her boyfriend, Jamiroquai singer Jay Kay.

Pregnancy chic: Melanie Blatt of All Saints shows off her bump during this summer's Party in the Park in London.

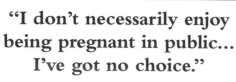

Top of the pops: 16-year-old Billie Piper twice headed the singles chart in the course of the year.

"I don't necessarily enjoy being pregnant in public... I've got no choice."

All Saints singer Melanie Blatt

Mother and daughter: Jerry Hall with Elizabeth Scarlett, who modelled for Mugler this summer.

Hard man: Footballer Vinnie Jones made a successful start in movies, playing an enforcer in Lock, Stock and Two Smoking Barrels.

Male leads: Matt Damon and Ben Affleck wrote and starred in the surprise hit film, Good Will Hunting.

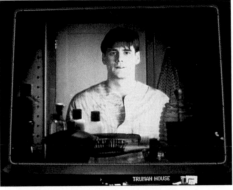

Film of the year: The Truman Show starred Jim Carrey as a man whose life was a full-time TV sitcom.

Missing out: Leonardo DiCaprio and Kate Winslet starred in the Oscar record-breaker Titanic, but didn't win Oscars themselves.

"Simply the world's biggest heart-throb."

Vanity Fair on Leonardo DiCaprio.

Shock frock: James Major, ex-prime minister's son, with fiancée Emma Noble.

Royal stud: Princess Anne's daughter Zara Phillips appears with a pierced tongue.

No longer with us

Michael Hutchence, lead singer of top Australian band INXS, died in Sydney.

Linda McCartney, wife of former Beatle Sir Paul, lost her long battle against cancer.

Famous Hollywood film cowboy Roy Rogers died in California aged 86.

Archbishop Trevor Huddleston was a founder of the Anti-Apartheid Movement.

Crooner Frank Sinatra spent more than three decades at the top of his profession.

Sonny Bono, singing partner of Cher in the 1960s, was killed in a skiing accident.

Longstanding country music favourite Tammy Wynette died aged 56. She was best known for songs such as D-i-v-o-r-c-e and her biggest hit, Stand By Your Man.

Ted Hughes, the Poet Laureate since 1984, died when at the height of his powers.

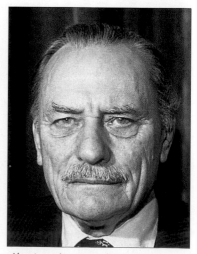
Abrasive right-wing politician Enoch Powell died from Parkinson's disease.

Chronicle 98

A year of news as it happened

Mid–November 1997
to mid–November 1998

How Chronicle 98 works

Chronicle 98 presents events from mid-November 1997 to mid-November 1998 as reported in the media at the time they happened. It allows you to follow events as they unfolded through the year. Many stories are linked to follow-up items identified by date. The links look like this: (→ May 20). They lead either to an entry in the news-in-brief panels or to one of the fuller news reports.

November

Exeter, 16
Fourteen-year-old Kate Bushell is found murdered in a field near her home on the outskirts of Exeter.

Elland Road, 16
The Great Britain rugby league team are beaten 20-37 by Australia in the third international of the British Gas series.

London, 18
Troubled Premiership football club Tottenham Hotspur appoints Christian Gross, Swiss coach of Zurich Grasshopper, as its new manager. (→ September 5)

Hollywood, 19
News leaks from Hollywood reveal that Diana, Princess of Wales, was considering a break into the movie business. It is alleged that she was to star with American actor Kevin Costner in a film about bodyguards.

Glasgow, 19
Rangers and England midfielder Paul Gascoigne is sent off during the Celtic-Rangers derby match after allegedly striking Celtic's Morten Wieghorst.

Westminster, 19
The Lord Chancellor, Lord Irvine, faces criticism after it is revealed that the refurbishment of his official residence has to date cost almost £333,000.

London, 19
An armed gang steals jewels and precious metals worth millions of pounds from a Cartier workshop in New Bond Street.

Beckenham and Winchester, 20
Two parliamentary by-elections bring no comfort to the Conservatives. They hold the safe seat of Beckenham, but with a much reduced majority. In Winchester, the Liberal Democrats turn a contested majority of just two votes in the general election into a majority of 21,000.

Seoul, 21
The South Korean government asks for a $20 billion loan from the IMF to shore up its failing economy. (→ November 23)

DEATHS
November 16. Saul Chaplin, Hollywood songwriter and film producer, the man behind musicals such as *An American in Paris* and *West Side Story*, dies aged 85.

November 18. Joyce Wethered (Lady Heathcoat Amory), the leading woman golfer of the 1920s, dies aged 96.

LONDON, THURSDAY 20
Queen celebrates golden wedding

Fifty years ago today, the 21-year-old Princess Elizabeth married Philip Mountbatten, newly created Duke of Edinburgh, in a ceremony of great splendour at Westminster Abbey. The anniversary of the occasion was celebrated in the more relaxed style of the contemporary monarchy.

The day began with a solemn thanksgiving service in Westminster Abbey. Then the Queen and Prince Philip proceeded slowly on foot up Whitehall, chatting to members of the crowd. After dropping in at No. 10 Downing Street, they walked to the Banqueting House, where a "people's banquet" was hosted by Prime Minister Tony Blair.

The banquet was so-named because a small number of "ordinary people" had been invited along with the celebrities. The guests included Lawrie Dennis, a car worker from Gateshead, and Helen James, a student and Guide leader. They heard the Queen express a debt of gratitude to the Duke of Edinburgh "greater than he would ever claim."

The day ended with a private ball at the newly restored Windsor Castle.

The Queen and Prince Philip stepping out together after 50 years of marriage.

Windsor, Monday 17. The last touches are applied to the restoration of Windsor Castle, five years after it was partially destroyed by fire. The restoration, which cost £37 million, has been completed ahead of schedule, in time for the Queen's golden wedding celebrations.

SYDNEY, SATURDAY 22
Bizarre death of pop star Hutchence

Michael Hutchence, lead singer of the successful Australian rock band INXS, was found dead in a hotel room at the Ritz-Carlton hotel in Sydney this morning. He was apparently hanging by his belt.

Hutchence, aged 37, was perhaps best known for his girlfriends, who included singer and actress Kylie Minogue, model Helena Christensen, and, over the last three years, former TV presenter Paula Yates. Hutchence recently announced that he and Yates were to marry in the near future.

Yates flew to Sydney this evening with their baby daughter Tiger Lily. Hutchence was reported to have been upset by an ongoing wrangle over custody of Yates's other children, by her ex-husband Bob Geldof. But friends expressed disbelief at the idea that Hutchence might have wanted to kill himself. (→ November 27)

EGYPT, MONDAY 17

Tourists massacred at ancient temple

Six Britons were among 58 tourists killed today in a terrorist attack at Luxor's Temple of Hatshepsut in the Valley of the Kings, one of Egypt's most popular tourist sites. The British dead included three generations of the Turner family from Ripponden, Yorkshire – five-year-old Shaunnah, her mother, and her grandmother.

The terrorists are believed to be Islamic extremists opposed to the Egyptian government of President Mubarak. They opened fire in the courtyard of the ancient temple at 9 a.m., just as tourists were turning up for a morning's sightseeing. They then hijacked two tourist buses, gunning down the passengers.

Egyptian security forces were soon on the scene and exchanged fire with the terrorists. Some were pursued to the nearby Valley of the Queens. Six terrorists and three Egyptian policemen are reported to have died in the fighting.

The outrage is the worst yet in a series of attacks on tourists by Islamic extremists in Egypt. It will be a devastating blow to the Egyptian tourist industry. (→ November 28)

An Egyptian soldier keeps guard over the Giza pyramids, Egypt's prime tourist spot, as Islamic extremists threaten more terror attacks.

Bristol, Wednesday 19. Pop star Gary Glitter has been quizzed by police about child pornography after technicians repairing his computer allegedly discovered suspect photos. (→ March 30)

WESTMINSTER, SUNDAY 16

Blair claims he is "a pretty straight sort of guy"

Prime Minister Tony Blair today appealed for the support of the British people after the most serious threat to his personal reputation since taking office. Accusations of corruption arose because of a possible link between a £1 million donation to Labour Party funds by Formula One boss Bernie Ecclestone and government backing for the exemption of Formula One from a European ban on tobacco advertising in sport.

Interviewed on BBC's *On The Record*, Blair apologised for mishandling the affair, but said he was "hurt and upset" that people might have thought his motives corrupt. Asking people to trust him, he said: "I think most people who have dealt with me think I'm a pretty straight sort of guy – and I am." (→ November 23)

IOWA, WEDNESDAY 19

"Iowa Seven" likely to survive

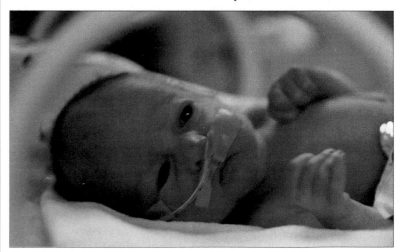

Kenneth Robert McCaughey, one of the Iowa septuplets, shortly after birth.

Bobbi McCaughey, from the small town of Carlisle, Iowa, has become the mother of septuplets. The seven babies were born at Iowa Methodist Medical Center, Des Moines. If they live, they will be the first septuplets ever to survive. Doctors tonight declared themselves "hopeful".

All the babies weighed over 2lb at birth, and two were over 3lb. The mother had been taking a fertility drug to aid conception.

November

Westminster, 23
The Labour Party announces that it is to give the £1 million donation it received from Formula One racing boss Bernie Ecclestone to a cancer charity.

Westminster, 25
In his first draft budget as Chancellor of the Exchequer, Gordon Brown provides £400 million to help pensioners with winter fuel bills and £300 million for after-school child-care clubs.

New York, 25
British television takes four out of six International Emmy awards, including the best drama award for BBC2's political satire *Crossing the Floor*.

Westminster, 25
The National Union of Teachers calls for a government inquiry into boys' educational failure after a national survey of 14-year-olds shows girls out-perform the opposite sex in almost every subject.

Westminster, 28
The House of Commons approves Michael Foster's bill to ban hunting with dogs by 411 votes to 151. However, the government is unlikely to give the bill sufficient parliamentary time for it to become law. (→ March 1)

Halifax, 28
Halifax coroners launch a worldwide search for the body of Luxor massacre victim Karina Turner, after the remains returned to Yorkshire are revealed not to be hers. The body of Karina's mother, also killed in the massacre, were earlier confused with those of a Swiss victim and sent to Zurich. (→ January 13)

Westminster, 29
Paymaster-General Geoffrey Robinson is alleged to be a possible beneficiary of an offshore tax-haven trust holding shares worth £12.5 million. (→ December 2)

Melbourne, 30
British golfer Lee Westwood beats Greg Norman in a sudden-death play-off to win the Australian Open.

DEATHS
November 25. Hastings Kamuzu Banda, president of Malawi from independence in 1964 to 1994, dies aged 91.

November 29. Kathy Acker, American writer, novelist, and performance artist, dies aged 53.

CAPE TOWN, SATURDAY 29

Spencer embroiled in divorce row

Earl Spencer, the brother of Diana, Princess of Wales, has been accused of serial adultery in a bitter divorce case that is being fought out in a South African court.

Countess Spencer alleges that her husband has had affairs with up to a dozen women since their marriage in 1989. Those backing Lady Spencer's allegations include Chantal Collopy, the ex-wife of a South African businessman, who herself claims to have had a relationship with the earl.

Earl Spencer has strenuously denied the allegations. His spokeswoman said he "wants to put the record straight and clear his name." The earl's current partner, former model Josie Borain, has also publicly defended his character against what she described as "bitter attacks".

Countess Spencer is attempting to have the divorce case transferred to a British court, which she believes will grant a more generous financial settlement. She is claiming £3.75 million. Earl Spencer has reportedly offered a £300,000 lump sum and £30,000 a year. (→ December 1)

Earl Spencer outside court in Cape Town, where he is fighting a bitter divorce case.

BRITAIN, THURSDAY 27

World's warmest year – but Britain may freeze

A Met Office report released today suggests that 1997 will turn out to be the warmest year ever recorded. Scientists estimate that the temperature of the Earth in 1997 will be 0.43°C above the average for 1961–90. This may not sound a lot, but if global warming continues, hundreds of millions of people may be menaced by floods or drought by 2050.

But the British shouldn't rush to order a lifetime supply of sun cream. According to oceanographer Wallace Broecker of Columbia University, New York, one possible effect of global warming could be to turn off the Gulf Stream, which is chiefly responsible for Britain's mild climate. If he is right, Britain could face a future of Arctic temperatures while much of the rest of the Earth bakes.

SOUTH LONDON, MONDAY 24

Downing Street cat alive and well

Humphrey appears content at his photo call, given at a secret location in South London.

After the announcement two weeks ago that Humphrey, the Downing Street cat, was retiring from public life, rumours began to circulate that he had been done away with on the orders of an allegedly cat-hating Cherie Blair. Today, the Blairs acted to rebut this slur. A photographer and camera crew were ferried to Humphrey's secret retirement home in a south London suburb, where they duly certified him alive and well.

Winnie Mandela confronts murder gang victims

Protected by a phalanx of bodyguards, Mrs Mandela arrives at the hearing in Johannesburg.

Winnie Madikizela-Mandela, the ex-wife of South African president Nelson Mandela, underwent public humiliation today as a string of witnesses accused her of violent crimes.

Winnie Mandela had been summoned to attend the Truth and Reconciliation Commission, which has been investigating South Africa's apartheid past. She seemed unmoved as distressed relatives of victims spoke of her part in alleged beatings and killings carried out in the late 1980s by her bodyguards, the "Mandela United Football Club".

She has denied all the allegations, but observers believe her reputation is now ruined. (→ December 4)

London, Friday 28. Singer Elton John put 10,000 items of his clothing on sale today at his Mayfair charity shop. The estimated proceeds of £250,000 will go to his Aids Foundation.

Atlantic rowers set 41-day record

Two New Zealand rowers, Phil Stubbs and Rob Hamill, have won a transatlantic rowing race in record time. Aboard their 23-foot boat *Kiwi Challenge*, the pair took 41 days to cover the 2,900 miles from Tenerife in the Canary Islands to Port St Charles, Barbados. This beat the existing transatlantic rowing record by an astonishing 32 days.

The Atlantic Rowing Race is organized by Sir Chay Blyth. Twenty-eight teams set out on the crossing, but Stubbs' and Hamill's nearest competitors are still 600 miles behind in the middle of the Atlantic Ocean.

Nurse in Saudi prison weds

British nurse Lucille McLauchlan, currently serving a prison term in Saudi Arabia, was married today in a courthouse in Damman, under the watchful eye of Saudi guards. She had been engaged to her husband, Grant Ferrie, for five years.

Last year McLauchlan was sentenced to eight years in prison and 500 lashes after she was found guilty of being an accessory to the murder of an Australian nursing colleague, Yvonne Gilford. (→ May 21)

Japanese securities house crash deepens Asian gloom

The Japanese corporation Yamaichi, one of the 10 largest securities houses in the world, has collapsed into bankruptcy. With its subsidiary companies, Yamaichi is thought to have debts of around £14 billion.

The collapse of Yamaichi is another devastating blow to the struggling Japanese economy. Japan's most powerful neighbour, South Korea, is also in the grip of a financial crisis and last week applied to the IMF for a loan of $20 billion. Western leaders are desperate to prevent the financial "Asian flu", which has brought chaos to Thailand, Indonesia, and Malaysia, from pushing the whole world economy into recession. (→ December 3)

Sydney, Thursday 27. Paula Yates (centre) arrives at St Andrew's Cathedral with her friend Belinda Brewin, and carrying her daughter Tiger Lily, for the funeral of her intended husband, singer Michael Hutchence. The service was also attended by Hutchence's ex-girlfriend, Kylie Minogue. (→ December 12)

Cape Town, 1
Earl and Countess Spencer agree a surprise out-of-court divorce settlement of £2 million and drop allegations made against each other. (→ October 5)

London, 2
Artist Gillian Wearing, 34, wins the £20,000 Turner Prize for her video work, including a recording of three rows of police officers sitting still for an hour.

Seoul, 3
The IMF and South Korea agree a multi-billion dollar loan package to bail out the South Korean economy.

Johannesburg, 4
At a session of the South African Truth and Reconciliation Commission, Winnie Mandela faces renewed accusations of involvement in the death of Stompie Moeketsi Seipei, a youth murdered in 1988 after being abducted by the "Mandela United Football Club".

Marseilles, 4
The draw for the opening round of the football World Cup finals next summer places the England team in Group G with Romania, Colombia, and Tunisia. Scotland are to play Brazil in the opening match of the finals.

London, 8
Five-day-old Baebhen Schuttke becomes Britain's youngest transplant patient. She is given a new liver in an operation at King's College Hospital, south London.

London, 8
Radio and TV presenter Chris Evans buys Virgin Radio from Richard Branson in an £80m deal.

Essex, 8
Mother-of-three Denise Giddings, 33, is charged with the abduction of baby Karli Hawthorne from a cot in the maternity unit at Basildon General Hospital on 5 December. Karli was three hours old at the time of the abduction.

London, 12
DNA testing confirms that Paula Yates is the daughter of dead television presenter Hughie Green. (→ February 5)

DEATHS
December 6. George Chisholm, OBE, jazz trombonist and humorist, dies aged 82.

December 7. Billy Bremner, Leeds and Scotland midfielder and manager at Leeds and Doncaster, dies aged 54.

London, Thursday 4. Visiting the offices of *The Big Issue*, the London magazine sold by the homeless, Prince Charles unexpectedly meets an old school chum, Clive Harold. Now down on his luck, Harold attended Hill House prep school with the Prince in the 1950s.

MARRAKESH, DECEMBER 10
Branson's record hopes float away

Tycoon Richard Branson's latest attempt to balloon non-stop around the world has been thwarted. Five hours before take-off, a freak gust of wind snapped the guy ropes and sent the helium-filled balloon drifting off towards Algeria – without Branson. Within an hour, the balloon had climbed to a height of 25,000 feet and began to drift idly across Moroccan and Algerian airspace.

It was being tracked by a Virgin jet as plans were put in place to salvage it. Engineers estimated that the vast balloon was capable of floating for three days and could pose a threat to other aircraft. After some hours, however, the runaway balloon came down in south west Algeria.

Branson himself is remaining optimistic about his latest setback. "I will do this again," he insists, "but next time I plan to be in the balloon."

WESTMINSTER, THURSDAY 20
Adams makes history at No. 10

Sinn Fein president Gerry Adams made history today when he became the first Republican leader to enter Downing Street in 76 years.

Mr Adams and six Sinn Fein MPs were greeted with cries of "murderers" and "New Labour, new traitors" from hostile crowds as they arrived at No. 10. But Prime Minister Tony Blair defended the meeting, saying the government should take "every risk it can" to secure peace.

At the Cabinet table, Mr Blair offered Mr Adams "a choice of history – violence and despair, or peace and progress." The symbolism of the event would not have been lost on the Sinn Fein leader: the last Irish Republican leader to enter the Cabinet office was Michael Collins, father of the IRA, when he negotiated the Irish partition with Prime Minister Lloyd George in 1921.

For his part, Mr Adams told the prime minister, politely but firmly, that it was time for Britain to leave Northern Ireland. After the meeting, Mr Adams called it "a moment in history", punching the air as he walked away. (→ December 28)

The Sinn Fein delegation at No. 10 includes Gerry Adams (right) and Martin McGuinness.

Royal tears as Britannia's 44-year service ends

The Queen, in red, walks down Britannia's gangplank for the final time. Royal Yachtsmen are lined up along the yacht's three decks.

The Queen dabs her eyes at the ceremony.

The Queen was visibly emotional today as the Royal Yacht *Britannia* was decommissioned, after 44 years of service to its country.

Prince Philip, Prince Charles, and the Princess Royal were among the 15-strong royal delegation at the short ceremony at South Railway Jetty in Portsmouth harbour.

In September, the Queen agreed to a Treasury request that there be no new Royal Yacht. The ageing *Britannia* cost £10m to run last year, and would have cost £60m to replace. It may now undergo a refit in the port of Leith, Edinburgh.

WESTMINSTER, TUESDAY 2

It's goodbye Tessa and hello Isa

Geoffrey Robinson, the Paymaster-General, today outlined a series of government proposals designed to transform the way British people invest their savings.

Out will go the tax-free Peps and Tessas introduced by the Tories in the 1980s. They are to be replaced by Isas – individual savings accounts – meant to attract even the low-paid into regular tax-free saving.

The most controversial aspect of the proposals is a £50,000 limit on tax-free savings. Mr Robinson said those affected were "well-off by most people's judgement". Tory speakers responded that people with £50,000 saved were not rich – unlike Mr Robinson, who is a multimillionaire. The Paymaster-General is currently under attack in the press over his financial affairs. (→ March 17)

Paris, December 1. Stephane Grappelli, jazz violinist, has died aged 89. His career spanned almost 50 years. He played with many great musicians, including Sir Yehudi Menuhin. His greatest musical partnership, however, was with Belgian gipsy guitarist Django Reinhardt.

WESTMINSTER, WEDNESDAY 3

Ban on T-bone steak revives British beef crisis

The government has announced a ban on the sale of beef on the bone after new scientific evidence that BSE – "mad cow disease" – could be spread through bone marrow. The ban will apply to products such as T-bone steaks, ribsteaks, and oxtails.

Announcing the ban, Agriculture Minister Jack Cunningham said there was a "very small risk" that beef on the bone might cause CJD (Creutzfeldt-Jakob Disease) in humans. He declared the government's determination to guarantee consumers "the highest protection possible" against the disease.

The surprise move is sure to outrage beef farmers, whose incomes have plummeted since the CJD crisis began in 1996. (→ February 12)

December

Death of "King Rat" sparks revenge

S	M	T	W	T	F	S
	1	2	3	4	5	6
7	8	9	10	11	12	13
14	15	16	17	18	19	20
21	22	23	24	25	26	27
28	29	30	31			

London, 14
British tennis No. 1 Greg Rusedski is named as Sports Personality of the Year in the BBC's *Sports Review of the Year*. No. 2 Tim Henman is named runner-up.

London, 15
Prince Charles attends the charity opening of the first Spice Girls movie *Spiceworld* at the Empire, Leicester Square, with sons William and Harry and their chums.

Durham, 18
Moors murderer Myra Hindley vows to fight on after she fails to overturn Home Secretary Jack Straw's decision that she must stay in prison until she dies.

London, 19
The High Court upholds an order for Tesco heiress Dame Shirley Porter to pay £27million in surcharges in the "homes-for-votes" Westminster housing scandal.

Britain, 21
The Spice Girls knock the Teletubbies off the perch for Christmas No. 1 with their single *Too Much*. (→ January 25)

Britain, 22
Experts warn that the country is suffering the worst outbreak of meningitis for half a century.

White Hart Lane, 22
German striker Jürgen Klinsmann is back at Tottenham – two and a half years after walking away – on a £175,000 deal from Sampdoria. He promises to do all he can to revive the ailing club.

Venice, 23
Film director Woody Allen, 62, weds girlfriend Soon-Yi Previn, 27, in a secret ceremony. The bride is the adopted daughter of Allen's former lover Mia Farrow and conductor André Previn.

London, 31
Singer Elton John is given a knighthood in the New Year's Honours List. Among the sports honours, retired footballer Tom Finney gets a knighthood, while former England bowler Alf Gover gains an MBE.

Ardersier, Scotland, 31
Actress Helen Mirren, 51, marries her long-term partner, American film director Taylor Hackford, in a Highland church.

DEATHS
December 31. Michael Kennedy, middle son of the late Senator Robert Kennedy, dies after suffering massive head injuries in a skiing accident, aged 39.

Ulster faces the threat of renewed sectarian violence after the murder yesterday morning of the Protestant paramilitary leader Billy Wright inside the Maze prison.

Wright, known as "King Rat", was head of the outlawed Loyalist Volunteer Force (LVF). He was shot by three fellow prisoners belonging to the Republican Irish National Liberation Army (INLA).

Within hours of Wright's death, LVF gunmen opened fire on a crowded hotel in Dungannon, County Tyrone, killing a Catholic man, Seamus Dillon, and wounding three others. (→ January 10)

LVF paramilitaries pose beside the body of their murdered leader, Billy Wright.

Minister's son falls into press drug trap

The son of a senior Labour Cabinet minister has been arrested for selling cannabis. Neither the youth nor his father can be named at present because of legal restrictions on the reporting of cases involving minors.

The case arose after Dawn Alford, a *Mirror* journalist, received a tip-off that a politician's son was involved with drugs. She met the youth in a south London pub and bought a quantity of cannabis from him. When the *Mirror* told the minister what had happened, he took his son to the police. (→ January 2)

England cricketers win desert war

England today won the Champions Cup, a one-day international cricket competition, held in the unlikely location of Sharjah, part of the United Arab Emirates.

England were elated by their three-wicket victory over the West Indies in the final. The one-day side captain, Adam Hollioake, said: "If anyone needed justification that specialist one-day sides are the way to go, we provided it."

Carlos the Jackal caged for life

Illich Ramirez Sanchez, better known as Carlos the Jackal, was today sentenced to life imprisonment by a French court. The most famous terrorist of his time, Carlos was responsible for the notorious kidnapping of 11 Opec oil ministers at a Vienna summit in 1975, as well as numerous bombings and killings. His conviction today was for the murder of two French secret service agents and an informer in 1975.

Carlos cut a poor figure in court, delivering rambling political speeches and abusing his own defence team as well as the presiding magistrates.

New York, Friday 19. After taking a fall in the first round, Naseem Hamed (right) successfully defended his WBO world featherweight title at Madison Square Gardens tonight. Hamed knocked out the challenger, Kevin Kelley of the United States, in round four.

Hague is wed but Tories are still blue

In the political wedding of the year, William Jefferson Hague married Ffion Llywelyn Jenkins at 2.38 this afternoon in the Chapel of St Mary Undercroft, the crypt chapel of the Palace of Westminster.

As is traditional, the Conservative leader was kept waiting before the ceremony, with the bride arriving 10 minutes late. After the service, in which the bride chose not to promise to obey her husband, the couple exchanged their vows in Welsh as well as English, ending by saying "Gwnaf", the Welsh for "I do". The new Mrs Hague was generally declared stunning in a sheath dress by designer Neil Cunningham.

Political observers are agreed that the Conservative Party was in sore need of an injection of glamour. A MORI opinion poll published in *The Times* yesterday showed Labour still maintaining a crushing lead over the Tories after eight months in power. Fifty-five per cent of those questioned said they would vote for Labour in a general election, while only 26 per cent declared their support for Mr Hague's party.

Wedded bliss: The bride and groom smile for cameras on the steps of the House of Commons.

Lamb called Polly in medical leap

The Roslin Research Institute in Midlothian, which last year made history with a cloned sheep called Dolly, has once more hit the headlines. Today the Institute's scientists showed off their latest achievement, a lamb called Polly, which has been genetically altered so that it produces a protein used to treat haemophilia. Scientists believe the protein may save thousands of human lives.

Britain, Monday 15. As supplies of Teletubby dolls fail to match demand, Christmas shoppers are gripped by Teletubby fever, buying armfuls when they can.

Disabled protesters challenge government over benefit cuts

Disabled people protest outside Downing Street, using red paint and handcuffs. A dozen were arrested but later released.

In a graphic protest against possible cuts in disability benefits, severely disabled protesters today handcuffed themselves to the Downing Street gates and splashed red paint around. There were 12 arrests.

The protests were provoked by reports that the government's current welfare reforms might include reducing or ending payments to disabled people considered well-off, and stricter rules controlling who can claim to be disabled.

The government insists that its welfare reforms are meant to target money to those in greatest need. In an interview with *The Times* newspaper, Chancellor of the Exchequer Gordon Brown robustly defended the government's policies, asserting that the "war against poverty in Britain can only be won by the modernizers". But the disabled continue to fear they will be chosen as a "soft target" for possible cuts.

S	M	T	W	T	F	S
				1	2	3
4	5	6	7	8	9	10
11	12	13	14	15	16	17
18	19	20	21	22	23	24
25	26	27	28	29	30	31

London, 2
Television "golden girl" Anthea Turner, 37, announces she has left her manager-cum-husband Peter Powell for the entrepreneur and married father of three, Grant Bovey.

Krasnodar, Russia, 5
American millionaire Steve Fossett is forced to abandon his fourth around-the-world balloon attempt, due to low winds and equipment malfunction. He had set off from St Louis, Missouri on December 31, heading east. (→ January 29)

Northamptonshire, 5
Thousands of people fail to get through on a telephone line that opened to take bookings to see the island grave of Diana, Princess of Wales, at Althorp. Despite this problem, an estimated 10,000 tickets are sold before 4.30 p.m. in the afternoon.

Northern Ireland, 11
Catholic Terry Enright, 28, the husband of Gerry Adam's niece, is killed in an attack on a Belfast nightclub by gunmen from the Loyalist Volunteer Force. Members claim the killing was in retaliation for the murder of its leader, Billy Wright, in the Maze on December 27. (→ February 10)

Brazil, 12
Outstanding Brazilian striker Ronaldo is voted World Football Player of the Year for the second time in succession. He wins with a landslide of 480 points awarded by an international consortium of 121 coaches.

Germany, 13
The body of Halifax woman Karina Turner, killed in the massacre at Luxor on November 17, is found in Germany.

London, 14
Former English football coach Terry Venables is banned from holding company directorships for seven years following his involvement in alleged bogus deals.

DEATHS
January 5. Sonny Bono, the pop singer turned Republican politician, dies in a skiing accident at Lake Tahoe, aged 62.

January 8. Sir Michael Tippett CBE, one of the greatest British musicians of this century, dies aged 93.

January 11. John Wells, satirist, actor, and playwright, who wrote the *Dear Bill* letters in *Private Eye* along with Richard Ingrams, dies aged 61.

WASHINGTON, D.C., SAT. 17

Clinton faces sex accuser Paula Jones

US President Bill Clinton, the most powerful man in the world, was today forced to sit face-to-face with a woman who is accusing him of sexual harassment. Paula Jones claims that Clinton, then a state governor, exposed himself to her in a hotel room in Arkansas in 1991.

In Jones's presence, the president gave six hours of testimony presenting his version of events. He claims to have no memory of ever having encountered Ms Jones. (→ January 21)

WALES, THURSDAY 15

Woman becomes mother at 60

A woman living in a country district of Wales has been revealed as Britain's oldest mother to give birth without having received fertility treatment. The mother, Elizabeth Buttle, was at first reported to be 54, but she is now known to be aged 60.

The baby, Joseph, was born last November. The mother has allegedly sold her story to a Sunday newspaper for an undisclosed sum.

Malmesbury, Friday 16. The second of two Ginger Tamworth pigs that escaped while being delivered to a slaughterhouse 10 days ago has been recaptured. The hunt for the Tamworth Two received worldwide media attention and led to them being bought by the *Daily Mail*. They will live out their days peacefully in an animal sanctuary.

NORTHERN IRELAND, SATURDAY 10

Mowlam enters the Maze in search for peace

Loyalist leaders Sam McGrory (left) and Michael Stone wait to meet Mo Mowlam.

The Northern Ireland Secretary Mo Mowlam proved yesterday that there are no limits to the government's search for peace in Ulster. She took the unprecedented step of visiting the Maze prison outside Belfast for talks with Protestant paramilitary leaders jailed for terrorist offences.

The prisoners had threatened to derail the peace process by refusing to sanction the participation of militant Unionist parties in talks planned for next week. Mowlam hoped to persuade them to sanction the talks.

Many people queried the wisdom of Mowlam going to meet gunmen and murderers, but today there is every sign that her gamble has paid off. The prisoners have agreed, at least temporarily, to give the peace talks a chance. (→ January 11)

Straw's son named in drugs case

Jack Straw arrives home clutching a batch of newspapers containing reactions to his speech.

A High Court judge today lifted the ban on naming the Cabinet minister's son arrested for selling drugs just before Christmas. The press are now able to reveal that the youth was 17-year-old William Straw, son of the Home Secretary Jack Straw – a man whose opposition to the legalization of cannabis is well-known,

At a press conference, Mr Straw defended his action in turning his son over to the police: "When a child does wrong, I believe it to be the duty of a parent to act promptly," he said. "That is what I sought to do."

Mr Straw has not been asked to resign. His position has if anything been strengthened by his response to the incident. Police are unlikely to press charges against his son.

William Straw shows the strain of his new-found notoriety as he leaves the family home.

Scotland, Wednesday 6. Rangers football star Paul Gascoigne admits that his estranged wife Sheryl is divorcing him. Here they are pictured in happier times, with her two children from a previous marriage.

Weather veers from storm to warm

In the last two weeks, Britain has been experiencing some remarkable extremes of weather. Only a week ago, on 4 January, parts of the country were battered by some of the worst storms since the hurricane of 1987. Winds of up to 105mph lashed Wales and the south and west of England, bringing down power lines and tearing roofs off buildings.

Today, however, Britain basked in an unseasonal warmth, with temperatures rising as high as 17°C (63°F). Some of the highest temperatures were recorded in Scotland, where skiers despaired as snow melted.

Cook's private life comes under scrutiny

Foreign Secretary Robin Cook is on the defensive about his private life after the publication of revelations by his estranged wife.

In excerpts from a book by Linda McDougall, *Westminster Women,* Mrs Cook claims that her husband had several affairs during their 28-year marriage. She also criticizes the prime minister's press secretary, Alistair Campbell, for his part in the break-up of the marriage last year, after the press discovered her husband's relationship with his assistant Gaynor Regan. Campbell denies telling Cook to end his marriage when the story was about to break.

The foreign secretary has stated that he will marry Ms Regan as soon as he is divorced. (→ April 9)

Humorist Frank Muir dies

Frank Muir, one of the best-loved figures in British broadcasting for more than half a century, has died at his Surrey home at the age of 77.

Muir wrote comedy series for radio and television, often in partnership with Denis Norden. He was also a familiar face on panel games such as *Call My Bluff,* where his wit and charm were seen to full effect.

Frank Muir, pictured wearing his trademark pink bow tie, has died at his home aged 77.

S	M	T	W	T	F	S
				1	2	3
4	5	6	7	8	9	10
11	12	13	14	15	16	17
18	19	20	21	22	23	24
25	26	27	28	29	30	31

Geneva, 20

The United Nations weather agency reports that 1997 was the hottest year on record. Last year's average temperature was 0.44°C (0.8°F) above the average for the years 1961-90. (→ February 4)

London, 21

John Culshaw, a prankster from London's Capital Radio, gets through on the phone to Prime Minister Tony Blair by imitating Opposition leader William Hague. But Mr Blair twigs when the hoaxer calls him "Tony" – Mr Hague only ever addresses him formally.

Anfield, 21

A stunning goal by boy wonder Michael Owen gives Liverpool a 1-0 victory over Newcastle, putting them third in the Premiership behind Blackburn Rovers and Manchester United. It could also book the 18-year-old's place in Glenn Hoddle's World Cup team. (→ February 11)

London, 23

St Pancras Chambers, the Gothic-style frontispiece of St Pancras Station, is to be turned into a 300-bed hotel and 60 flats in a £60m scheme. It will also front the planned Eurostar terminus in London.

Cuba, 25

The Pope, at the end of the first ever visit by a pontiff to the Caribbean island of Cuba, calls on President Fidel Castro's Communist government to move towards a free democracy. (→ March 21)

London, 29

Sky Television drops Geoffrey Boycott from its commentary team for the Test series in the West Indies after a French court fines him for violence to an ex-lover. BBC's Radio Five Live also dropped the former Yorkshire and England batsman. (→ July 2)

DEATHS

January 19. Rock legend Carl Perkins, composer of *Blue Suede Shoes*, dies in Nashville, Tennessee, aged 65.

January 21. Jack Lord, American actor who starred in the long-running TV series *Hawaii Five-0*, dies aged 68.

January 23. Victor Passmore, "grand old man of British painting", dies at his home in Malta, aged 89.

January 26. Hogan "Kid" Bassey, MBE, Nigerian-born British boxer and world featherweight champion from 1957–59, dies in Lagos, aged 65.

Dreams come true: Stevenage's goalscorer, Giuliano Grazioli, celebrates his equaliser.

SWITZERLAND, THURSDAY 29
Brit launches round-the-globe bid from Alps

Another balloonist entered the race to become first to circumnavigate the globe non-stop today. British adventurer Andy Elson and his two crew launched their record bid from Château d'Oex in the Swiss Alps. If all goes to plan, they could arrive at their final destination in Algiers in 16 days' time. Elson, 44, became the first balloonist to fly over Mount Everest in 1991. (→ February 4)

LONDON, MONDAY 26
Queen Mother undergoes second hip operation

The Queen Mother was reported to be comfortable, but tired, in hospital last night, following an operation to replace a fractured left hip.

She sustained the injury yesterday afternoon, when she had a fall while she was visiting her seven brood mares at Sandringham. She was taken to the Edward VII Hospital for Officers in Marylebone, where it was decided she was robust enough to undergo a full hip operation.

The Queen Mother, who is 97 years old, had already had her right hip replaced, in 1995.

STEVENAGE, SUNDAY 25
Stevenage keep Cup magic alive

The FA Cup exploded with drama last night as Vauxhall Conference minnows Stevenage Borough held Premiership giants Newcastle United to a 1-1 draw at their tiny home ground, Broadhall Way.

It seemed a standard story when England captain Alan Shearer scored for Newcastle with only two minutes on the clock. But Stevenage tore up the script, giving Newcastle a fierce chasing and equalising three minutes before half-time. The second half was goalless, ensuring Stevenage a replay at St James' Park. (→ February 4)

Cheshire, Sunday 25. Hearts break all over Britain as Posh Spice Victoria Adams, 23, and star footballer David Beckham, 22, announce they are to wed. The pair, who have been together for 10 months, exchanged his-and-her diamond rings. (→ February 11)

WASHINGTON, D.C., WEDNESDAY 21

"Sex, lies, and tapes" scandal rocks the White House

White House intern Monica Lewinsky caught on old news footage with Mr Clinton. They began an illicit affair in 1995, she says.

Bill Clinton's presidency could be brought to its knees by an investigation that was launched today into whether he had an affair with a young White House intern, and then asked her to lie under oath about it.

Ten damning audio tapes have been handed to the independent prosecutor, Kenneth Starr, who was originally investigating the president over Whitewater land deals.

On the tapes, Monica Lewinsky, 24, apparently describes an 18-month affair with the president to a friend, Pentagon worker Linda Tripp – who was wired by Starr's investigators.

The tapes appear to contradict both Lewinsky's and the president's testimony in the Paula Jones case, denying that they had an affair. Even more damaging for the president, Lewinsky allegedly told Tripp she was pressured to testify falsely in the Paula Jones case. (→ January 26)

WASHINGTON, D.C., MON 26

Clinton fights back over Lewinsky scandal

President Bill Clinton last night upped the stakes in the political crisis swirling around him by issuing a total denial of charges of sexual and moral impropriety, on live television.

With his wife Hillary standing next to him, he hit back at claims he had an affair with Monica Lewinsky, a White House intern, and asked her to deny it under oath.

Emphasizing each word, he said: "I want to say one thing to the American people. I want you to listen to me. I'm going to say this again. I did not have sexual relations with that woman, Miss Lewinsky. I never told anyone to lie, not a single time, never. These allegations are false." Analysts say that if the claims now prove to be true, these words will damn him in the nation's eyes.

The president's legal position is perilous. If it is shown that he committed perjury, lied under oath, or put pressure on Lewinsky to perjure herself, then he could face impeachment or even a prison sentence.

Meanwhile, independent counsel Kenneth Starr is pushing the investigation forwards. He is preparing to subject a dress, said to bear traces of Clinton's semen, to DNA tests. And the Paula Jones sex-harassment case, due to begin on May 27, still hangs over the president. (→ February 5)

Hollywood, Monday 19. Dame Judi Dench, 63, wins the Golden Globe award for best actress for her role as the grieving Queen Victoria in the movie *Mrs Brown*.

LONDON, FRIDAY 23

Assault claim not cricket, says Boycott

Former England cricketer Geoffrey Boycott today denied assaulting his ex-lover Margaret Moore in a hotel in France in 1996. On Tuesday, a French court found in favour of Moore, issuing Boycott with a fine and a suspended sentence.

Boycott was not in court, and has been granted a retrial. He claims a "vindictive" Moore made the allegations because he wouldn't marry her. His career as a cricket commentator is now at risk. (→ January 29)

Boycott: ex-mistress's claim that he gave her two black eyes is "untrue", he tells press.

February

Brussels, 4
Bill Gates, head of Microsoft and America's richest man, is hit in the face with a custard pie while on a visit to Belgium. He is the latest victim of a group of Belgian pranksters who throw custard pies at celebrities they deem to be guilty of self-importance.

Newcastle, 4
Following a 1-1 draw on their home ground, gallant Stevenage fight valiantly against the might of Newcastle United at St James' Park, but lose 2-1 in the FA Cup fourth-round replay.

China, 4
British balloonist Andy Elson's attempt to fly around the world fails after the Chinese authorities refuse to allow him to fly through their airspace.

London, 4
A report in *Nature* magazine suggests that the HIV virus responsible for Aids first appeared in humans in Africa in the late 1940s. The virus was not identified until the 1980s, by which time Aids had already become a worldwide epidemic.

Washington, D.C., 5
On a trip to the United States, Prime Minister Tony Blair announces that the Queen is to honour comedian Bob Hope with an honorary knighthood in recognition of work entertaining troops during World War II.

Sydney, 5
An Australian coroner rules that singer Michael Hutchence, found hanged in a Sydney hotel last November, killed himself while suffering from depression.

Portsmouth, 6
Lieutenants Sue Moore and Melanie Rees, both aged 26, become the first women to be given command of Royal Navy warships, ending centuries of an exclusive male tradition. (→ March 19)

Japan, 7
The 18th Winter Olympic Games are declared open at Nagano with a lavish ceremony featuring giant globes, dancing girls, and Sumo wrestlers.

Paris, 7
England lose to France 24-17 in a Five Nations rugby union match held at the newly opened Stade de France.

DEATHS
February 2. Dr Robert McIntyre, the SNP's first member of parliament and later party leader, dies aged 84.

Old Trafford pays its respects to Busby's Babes

Manchester United players pause for a minute's silence during the ceremony to mark the 40th anniversary of the Munich air crash.

At 3.04 p.m. today 55,000 football fans, young and old alike, rose to their feet at Old Trafford for a minute's silence to honour Busby's Babes, the superb Manchester United team built up by the late Sir Matt Busby and all but wiped out in an air disaster 40 years ago. The plane bringing the team home from a match in Belgrade crashed at Munich airport while landing to refuel.

Sir Bobby Charlton, a survivor of the crash, was among the representatives of football clubs, relatives, friends, and supporters who laid wreathes on the pitch during the moving tribute. The minute's silence culminated in a heartfelt roar of pure emotion which echoed around the stadium. Manchester United went on to draw 1-1 with Bolton Wanderers.

Branson vindicated in case against lottery rival

A triumphant Richard Branson embraces his wife Joan after hearing the verdict.

Richard Branson, the Virgin entrepreneur, was jubilant today after a victory in the High Court that could fundamentally affect the future of the National Lottery.

A jury rejected a libel action brought against Branson by businessman Guy Snowden, a director of the National Lottery operator Camelot. Branson had alleged that Snowden attempted to bribe him to pull out of the race to run the National Lottery in 1994.

After the judgment, Snowden announced his resignation from the Camelot board. He is expected to pay damages of around £100,000 to Branson, plus legal costs that may total millions of pounds. The Virgin boss called for the establishment of a non-profit-making "people's lottery".

London, Sunday 1. *The Full Monty*, starring Robert Carlyle, wins best film of the year at the Evening Standard British Film Awards.

ITALY, TUESDAY 3

Cable car crashes after jet slices wire

At least 20 people were killed today when a low-flying American military aircraft sliced through the steel wire of a cable-car lift. The accident happened at the Italian ski resort of Cavalese, near Trento in the Dolomites. The cable car, which was carrying skiers up the mountain to the ski slopes, plunged about 100m (300ft) to the valley floor.

The aircraft, a US Marine Corps A-6B Prowler, was on a routine training flight when it apparently ran into technical trouble seconds before the accident happened. The pilot managed to return to his base at Aviano, where he made an emergency landing. US officials later reported that although he had felt a jolt, the pilot was unaware that the aircraft had collided with the cable.

Italian rescue workers survey the wreckage of the cable car lying on the slopes of Mount Cermis. There were no survivors of the accident.

UNITED STATES, WEDNESDAY 4

El Niño storms batter US

A storm blamed on the warming of the waters of the Pacific – the El Niño effect – has hit the west coast of the United States, bringing gale-force winds and torrential rain to much of California. A second storm, also blamed on El Niño, has caused chaos in the American south-east.

The El Niño effect is being blamed for disasters ranging from drought in Peru to forest fires in Indonesia. Some of the scientists monitoring the effect believe it is causing one of the most widespread natural disasters of all time.

WASHINGTON, D.C., THURS. 5

That "special relationship" continues

At the start of a three-day visit to Washington, British Prime Minister Tony Blair today stood next to President Bill Clinton outside the White House to give him Britain's wholehearted support for any US military confrontation with Iraq. Blair applauded Clinton's political achievements and brushed aside any mention of the Monica Lewinsky scandal now threatening the beleaguered president, as irrelevant to his performance as a world leader.

Los Angeles, Friday 6. Carl Wilson (centre), vocalist and guitarist with the Beach Boys, died of cancer today at the age of 51. He was the youngest of the three brothers who created the band in 1961.

TEXAS, TUESDAY 3

Karla Faye dies after 14 years in jail

Karla Faye Tucker, 38, today became the first woman to be put to death by the state of Texas since 1863. She was executed by lethal injection after serving 14 years on death row.

Tucker had been convicted of murdering a woman with a pick-axe in 1983. She had undergone a religious conversion while in prison, leading to worldwide appeals for clemency. But last-ditch attempts to secure a reprieve were turned down. Relatives of the murdered woman witnessed the execution in the Death House at Huntsville Prison.

S	M	T	W	T	F	S
1	2	3	4	5	6	7
8	9	10	11	12	13	14
15	16	17	18	19	20	21
22	23	24	25	26	27	28

Bristol, 9
Student David Frost is found guilty of murdering teenager Louise Smith in the early hours of Christmas Day 1996. Frost evaded arrest for 15 months but was trapped when a DNA sample that he provided proved to be a positive match.

London, 9
Bath prop forward Kevin Yates is given a six-month suspension by rugby union officials for biting the ear of London Scottish flanker Simon Fenn in a Tetley's Bitter Cup match in January.

Trinidad, 9
Carl Hooper, scorer of an unbeaten 94, inspires the West Indies cricketers to victory over England in the Second Test in Port of Spain. (→ February 17)

Northern Ireland, 10
Unionist leaders say that they will demand the expulsion of Sinn Fein from peace talks at Stormont if the IRA are implicated in the murders of Brendan Campbell and Robert Dougan, killed in Belfast over the last 24 hours. (→ February 20)

Afghanistan, 11
The first helicopter carrying aid manages to land in sub-zero temperatures in northern Afghanistan a week after a series of earthquakes devastated the area.

London, 11
Mohamed Al Fayed, the controversial Egyptian owner of Harrods, claims that the car crash in which his son Dodi and Diana, Princess of Wales, were killed, was not an accident. "I will not rest until I have established exactly what happened," Al Fayed declares. (→ June 5)

Paris, 11
American movie star Robert de Niro reacts angrily after he is questioned by French authorities investigating an international prostitution racket. His French lawyer insists that the actor has "never in his life paid a woman" for sex.

Scotland, 12
Scottish hotelier Jim Sutherland becomes the first person in Britain to be prosecuted for breaking the ban on beef on the bone imposed by the Government in December 1997. This follows a dinner held at Mr Sutherland's hotel south of Edinburgh in December in an apparently deliberate attempt to defy the ban. (→ April 21)

DEATHS
February 10. Maurice Schumann, French patriot, soldier, writer, and elder statesman, dies aged 86.

Prescott gets wet, wet, wet as Brit Awards honour All Saints

All Saints are hoping to replace the Spice Girls as Britain's top all-female group.

The annual Brit Awards show has become an occasion when gestures of protest are expected. The main victim this year was Deputy Prime Minister John Prescott, a guest at the ceremony, who was doused with ice-cold water by Danbert Nobacon of anarchist band Chumbawumba. Among award winners were All Saints, who won best single and best video for their record *Never Ever*. Finley Quaye was an unexpected choice for best male artist. The Verve were voted top British group.

Bhutan, Wednesday 11. The Prince of Wales takes time out for some watercolour sketching during a visit to the Himalayan state of Bhutan. The Prince has been mixing some relaxation with official functions during a tour of parts of the Indian subcontinent.

British actresses in line for Oscars

British stars have won four of the five places on the shortlist for best actress in this year's Academy Awards.

Kate Winslet is nominated for her role in *Titanic*, Helena Bonham Carter for *The Wings of the Dove*, and Julie Christie for her part in *Afterglow*. A "stunned" Dame Judi Dench is nominated for her portrayal of Queen Victoria in *Mrs Brown*, a role which has already won her a Golden Globe award. The British movie *The Full Monty* also has four nominations. (→ March 24)

Owen is England's youngest player

Owen, 18, joins the England squad.

At the age of 18 years and 59 days, Liverpool striker Michael Owen tonight became the youngest player to appear for the England football team this century. But his promising debut performance could not prevent a shock 0-2 home defeat for England at the hands of Chile.

The star of the match was the Chilean striker Marcelo Salas, scorer of both goals. Salas is now expected to be a key player in this summer's World Cup finals. Whether Owen will figure in the finals remains a matter for England coach Glenn Hoddle to ponder. (→ April 4)

STAMFORD BRIDGE, THURSDAY 12

Gullit shocked by Chelsea sacking

Former Dutch international Ruud Gullit, rejected by Chelsea despite making it the most fashionable club in British football.

The flamboyant Chelsea football club manager Ruud Gullit has been sacked by his club, allegedly over his demand for a new contract worth over £3 million a year.

Chelsea's abrasive chairman, Ken Bates, told a hastily convened press conference: "Football economics aren't yet that crazy." But Gullit said he was shocked by the dismissal, which he first heard of through Teletext. The Dutchman denied that there had been any negotiations over an expensive new contract.

Last year Gullit led Chelsea to victory in the FA Cup, and the team is currently in second place in the Premiership. But for some time rumours have been circulating of dissension in the Chelsea dressing room. A number of poor results, including a 3-5 home defeat by Manchester United in the FA Cup in January, had tarnished Gullit's reputation. Some commentators feel that the major issue is the manager's playboy lifestyle and his many outside business interests.

Chelsea's new manager will be their Italian striker Gianluca Vialli. Seeming a little bemused, Vialli described the new appointment as "unbelievable". (→ August 27)

New manager Gianluca Vialli, second from left, flanked by members of the Chelsea board.

LONDON, FRIDAY 13

Harman "the Horrible" hears his last case

Controversial High Court judge Mr Justice Harman resigned today as Court of Appeal judges criticized his "intolerable delay" of 20 months in deciding on a case. In a colourful career, Harman became well known for being out of touch with modern life. He famously asked, "Who is Gazza?" after the World Cup in 1990, and once said to a female witness, "I've always thought there were only three kinds of women: wives, whores, and mistresses. Which are you?"

London, Sunday 8. Charismatic and controversial politician Enoch Powell, best known for his "rivers of blood" speech given in April 1968, died today aged 85. He had suffered from Parkinson's disease for some time.

CHESHIRE, WEDNESDAY 11

The pose that cost Posh Spice dear

Vigilant customs officials took a more than passing interest when celebrity couple Posh Spice and David Beckham posed for the press displaying their engagement rings last month. The officials noticed that Beckham's ring, bought by Posh Spice during a recent visit to Hollywood, had not been declared on entry to this country. The embarrassed Spice Girl will now face a bill from customs of around £3,000.

27

S	M	T	W	T	F	S
1	2	3	4	5	6	7
8	9	10	11	12	13	14
15	16	17	18	19	20	21
22	23	24	25	26	27	28

Westminster, 15
Prime Minister Tony Blair criticizes the "tacky" exploitation of the memory of Diana, Princess of Wales, by the memorabilia industry.

Indonesia, 15
Five people are killed and dozens injured as unrest spreads throughout Indonesia. Much of the rioting is directed against the Chinese minority. (→ May 20)

London, 16
At the Olivier Awards, Ian Holm wins the best actor award for his King Lear. Zoe Wanamaker wins best actress with her performance in *Electra*.

Taiwan, 16
A Taiwanese airbus crashes while landing at Taipei airport in heavy rain. All 196 people on board are killed, as well as nine victims on the ground.

Westminster, 19
The House of Commons Home Affairs Select Committee formally orders the United Grand Lodge of England to hand over names of Freemasons involved in police corruption cases.

Twickenham, 21
England beat Wales 60-26 in the Five Nations rugby tournament, the highest aggregate score in the history of the competition. (→ April 4)

Lord's, 23
The MCC, England's top cricket club, votes to reject a proposal to admit women members. (→ September 28)

Barbados, 24
Princess Margaret undergoes tests in a Bridgetown hospital after suffering a mild stroke at her holiday home on Mustique.

City of London, 24
A proposed multi-billion pound merger between pharmaceutical giants Glaxo Wellcome and SmithKline Beecham collapses in acrimony, allegedly after disagreements between top managers.

Northern Ireland, 27
The Northern Ireland Court of Appeal quashes paratrooper Lee Clegg's conviction for the murder of a teenage girl joyrider shot dead at an army checkpoint in 1993, and orders a retrial.

DEATHS
February 16. Martha Gellhorn, the first female war correspondent, who covered the D-day landings, Vietnam, and the Arab-Israeli wars, dies in London aged 84.

LONDON, TUESDAY 24

Contents of the Dome unveiled

This computer graphic shows the giant figure intended to feature in the Millennium Dome.

Prime Minister Tony Blair today granted the press and business chiefs a glimpse of the projected contents of the controversial Millennium Dome currently under construction in Greenwich. The structure will include the largest model of the human body anywhere in the world, and a number of different "zones", such as "Dreamscape" and "Serious Play", dedicated to various areas of human creativity and values.

The prime minister told the select gathering in the Royal Festival Hall that the Dome, the centrepiece of Britain's celebration of the year 2000, would be "the envy of the world". But sceptics remain unconvinced that the millions of pounds being poured into the project are funds well spent. (→ June 22)

NORTHERN IRELAND, FRI. 20

Slap on the wrist for Sinn Fein angers Unionists

After many delays and hesitations, Sinn Fein was expelled from the multi-party Northern Ireland peace talks in Stormont today, but only for a period of two weeks. Sinn Fein's expulsion followed two murders in Northern Ireland last week attributed to the IRA. The maintenance of an IRA ceasefire is a condition of Sinn Fein participation in the talks.

Protesting at the brevity of the expulsion, Ulster Unionist leader David Trimble said: "It shows life is cheap." But the British and Irish governments remain determined to involve Sinn Fein in a settlement of the Ulster conflict. (→ March 3)

Tyneside, Sunday 15. Antony Gormley's massive steel sculpture *Angel of the North* rises above the A1 at Gateshead. Costing £800,000, the angel has been a subject of intense controversy since it was first mooted four years ago. Around 20m (60ft) tall and with roughly the wingspan of a jumbo jet, it is the largest sculpture in Britain.

LONDON, THURSDAY 19
Queen shows the common touch on East End visit

The Queen drops in for a chat with East Ender Eva Priest on a Hackney housing estate.

A pensioner in London's East End, 85-year-old Eva Priest, found herself entertaining the Queen of England in her one-bedroom flat today.

On a visit to Hackney's Kingshold Estate, the Queen chatted with Mrs Priest for a few minutes and posed for photographs. The delighted pensioner later told reporters: "I could have talked to her all day."

The visit was one episode in a concerted effort to update the image of the Royal Family in the wake of last year's death of Diana, Princess of Wales. Concerned not to appear remote from the people, the Queen has taken care to make contact with her subjects in their everyday lives.

BAGHDAD, SUNDAY 22
UN chief fixes Iraq peace deal

After weeks of sabre-rattling by the Western powers and defiant rhetoric from the Iraqi president, Saddam Hussein, peace has unexpectedly broken out in the Gulf.

Kofi Annan, the UN Secretary-General, announced that a peace deal had been agreed today. Annan had flown to the Iraqi capital, Baghdad, for emergency talks with Saddam, aimed at averting imminent air strikes by the United States and Britain.

The crisis had arisen over Iraq's failure to comply with the terms imposed after its defeat in the 1991 Gulf War. Iraq is supposed to allow UN inspectors access to any sites they wish to visit in the search for weapons of mass destruction.

Saddam had been blocking access to certain sites and generally obstructing the inspection process. This led the United States to prepare for attacks on targets inside Iraq, a policy fully supported by Britain.

American and British leaders gave a cautious welcome to news of the agreement. A Downing Street source said that Prime Minister Tony Blair wanted assurances that there would be "no concessions at all on matters of fundamental principle".

London, Friday 20. Model Honor Fraser flaunts the flag at the opening of London Fashion Week. The Union Jack was painted on to her body by make-up artist Tina Earnshaw. The week is to include 55 catwalk shows, exhibiting the cream of British fashion.

TRINIDAD, TUESDAY 17
Gutsy England scrape Test win

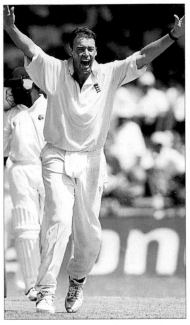

Man of the match Fraser dismisses Lara.

England's cricketers achieved a tense three-wicket victory in the Third Test against the West Indies at Port of Spain today. They scored 225 to win, largely thanks to an innings of 83 by opener Alec Stewart. England's other hero was bowler Angus Fraser, who took nine wickets in the match.

England captain Mike Atherton described the win as "a terrific test of character". The series is now level at one win apiece. (→ March 2)

OXFORD, WEDNESDAY 25
Circus worker mauled by tiger

A worker at Chipperfield Circus, 32-year-old Nigel Wesson, is recovering at the John Radcliffe Hospital in Oxford tonight after Rajah, a Bengali tiger, bit off his left arm below the elbow. The injured man remained in remarkably good spirits. When a hospital orderly asked him if he was allergic to anything, he wryly replied: "Only to tigers!"

The Chipperfield family was still coming to terms with a tragic incident last month in which a tiger closed its jaws on the head of Richard Chipperfield, a 24-year-old big-cat trainer. He is still in a coma.

S	M	T	W	T	F	S
1	2	3	4	5	6	7
8	9	10	11	12	13	14
15	16	17	18	19	20	21
22	23	24	25	26	27	28
29	30	31				

London, 2
The will of Diana, Princess of Wales, is published, revealing that she left almost £13 million to her sons Prince William and Prince Harry.

Guyana, 2
England's cricketers suffer a crushing 242-run defeat in the Fourth Test against the West Indies in Georgetown. The West Indies lead the series 2-1. (→ March 16)

Northern Ireland, 3
Catholic Damien Trainor and his lifelong Protestant friend Philip Allen are shot dead by Loyalist gunmen in a Catholic-owned bar in the village of Poyntzpass, County Armagh. (→ March 15)

Melbourne, 8
Finnish driver Mika Hakkinen wins the Australian Grand Prix, the first race of the Formula One season. His McLaren team-mate David Coulthard, in the lead, allows Hakkinen to beat him. (→ March 29)

Westminster, 9
Home Secretary Jack Straw frees Roisin McAliskey, daughter of former MP Bernadette McAliskey, on the grounds of her poor mental health. She was being held pending extradition to Germany, where she had been facing charges relating to an IRA attack on a British army base.

Luton, 11
Train driver Peter Afford is found not guilty of manslaughter. He had been accused of responsibility for the Watford rail crash of August 1996, in which one person died and 70 were injured.

Cambridge, Massachusetts, 12
American astronomers claim that an asteroid, dubbed XF11, is due to pass very close to the Earth in the year 2028.

Indian Wells, California, 13
Playing in the Newsweek Champions Cup, British tennis star Greg Rusedski sets a new world record with a serve of 146mph (234kph).

Old Trafford, 14
Arsenal beat the Premiership leaders Manchester United 0-1 with a goal from Dutchman Marc Overmars. The victory opens up a championship race that United had seemed sure to win. (→ May 3)

DEATHS
March 10. Lloyd Bridges, US film and TV actor, father of actor sons Beau and Jeff, dies in Los Angeles, aged 85.

EXETER, MONDAY 9
Babysitter scarred in "mistaken identity" attack

A jealous husband, Peter Humphrey, was sentenced to 12 years in prison at Exeter Crown Court today for ordering an acid attack that left a babysitter scarred for life.

The attack took place in Seaton, east Devon, in July 1996. Humphrey paid an unknown man to call at his house and throw nitric acid in his wife's face. But it was the babysitter, Beverley Hammett, who opened the door to the assailant.

Miss Hammett, now aged 21, has undergone a series of operations to rebuild her face after the devastating damage caused by the acid. Passing sentence, Judge Graham Cottle described the attack as an "evil act".

Birmingham, Sunday 8. Judy Averis of Cheadle, Staffordshire, poses with her Welsh Terrier, Mel, named best in show at this year's Crufts. A dog owned by Mrs Averis's father won the same honour in 1963.

KOSOVO, WEDNESDAY 11
The spectre of "ethnic cleansing" continues to haunt Serbia as the crisis in Kosovo worsens

Ethnic Albanian Muslims in the village of Prekaz mourn victims of a Serbian police massacre last week that cost 52 lives.

The Serbian government is under increasing international pressure to halt a crackdown in the Kosovo region that increasingly resembles the notorious "ethnic cleansing" of areas of Bosnia in the recent past.

The Serbian authorities have reacted angrily to demands for an independent Kosovo from ethnic Albanians, who form the majority of Kosovo's population. Today foreign journalists witnessed people in the village of Prekaz mourn 52 victims of the Serbian police massacre last week. Despite the imposition of sanctions by the Western powers, the Serbian government has refused to talk with Kosovan separatists. (→ June 7)

LONDON, SUNDAY 1

Green wellies and flat caps swamp London as the countryside protests

This was the day when the country came to town. Goaded by the perceived failure of the Government to take account of the concerns of rural dwellers, about a quarter of a million people responded to the call of the Countryside Alliance and flooded into London from all parts of the country. It was probably the largest demonstration in Britain this decade.

One major focus of the march was opposition to a possible ban on blood sports such as fox-hunting. But there were wider concerns, ranging from the prospect of more building on greenbelt land to the continuing row surrounding the handling of the "Mad Cow Disease" crisis. Protesters also called for an end to the decline of rural services such as village shops and country buses.

The Government says it is ready to listen to the countryside lobby. In particular, faced with such vocal opposition, a ban on hunting looks unlikely in the short term.

Countryside marchers wend their way from Victoria Embankment to Hyde Park.

LONDON, TUESDAY 3

Ceiling falls in on Palace guest

Nick Howell, 28, was watching an investiture ceremony at Buckingham Palace today when a chunk of plaster from the Palace ballroom ceiling fell on his head, knocking him to the floor. "It was a huge shock," Mr Howell said, "not what you expect to happen." The Queen, who was about 30m (100ft) away, continued with the ceremony unperturbed.

LONDON, TUESDAY 10

An end to Cool Britannia?

According to the influential music paper *New Musical Express*, New Labour has lost its appeal for the trendy young. A survey of top rock musicians, many of whom supported Tony Blair in last year's election, finds them at best cynical and at worst hostile. New Labour's "Cool Britannia" image is dismissed by *NME* as "a cute little brand name".

London, Sunday 1. Dermot Morgan, the actor famous for his role in the satirical TV sitcom *Father Ted*, died suddenly at his home in south London today. He was only 45 years old.

CALIFORNIA, THURSDAY 5

Space probe finds water on the Moon

Scientists working for the American space agency Nasa announced today that they have discovered evidence for the existence of considerable quantities of frozen water on the Moon. If it is confirmed, the discovery will open up the prospect of the use of the Moon as a base for exploration further into space.

The Nasa scientists have been studying data sent back by a space probe, *Lunar Prospector*, which is in orbit around the Moon. The information suggests that buried water is scattered around the lunar poles.

The water deposits could be used as a source of oxygen and hydrogen, the gases needed to make rocket fuel. Scientist Dr Alan Binder said: "For the first time we can go to a planetary body and we can fuel up. That fuel can be used to go to Mars or elsewhere in the solar system."

PARIS, WEDNESDAY 11

Paul and Linda attend daughter Stella's show for Chloë

Sporting anti-fur badges, Paul and Linda McCartney enjoy their daughter's big day.

Proud parents Sir Paul and Linda McCartney had front row seats for the French fashion house Chloë's show in Paris today – not surprising really, since the chief designer is their 26-year-old daughter Stella.

Stella dedicated the show, her second for Chloë, "to her mum". Linda, who was diagnosed with breast cancer in 1996, has only recently returned to the public eye following chemotherapy treatment. (→ April 17)

S	M	T	W	T	F	S
1	2	3	4	5	6	7
8	9	10	11	12	13	14
15	16	17	18	19	20	21
22	23	24	25	26	27	28
29	30	31				

Northern Ireland, 15
Loyalist David Keys, 26, arrested under suspicion of a dual murder at Poyntzpass two weeks ago, is killed in the Maze prison. His death initially appears to be suicide. (→ March 23)

India, 15
Following the Indian general elections last week, former foreign minister and political moderate, Atal Behari Vajpayee, is invited to form a coalition government.

Barbados, 16
With England in a winning position, rain washes out play on the last day of the Fifth Test against the West Indies in Bridgetown. The draw leaves the West Indies 2-1 up in the series with one match to play. (→ March 24)

London, 16
Buckingham Palace confirms that Camilla Parker Bowles, long-term close companion of the Prince of Wales, was among his house guests at Sandringham, the Queen's private residence, last weekend.

Jerusalem, 17
Visiting Israel on behalf of the European Union, Foreign Secretary Robin Cook is snubbed by Israeli Prime Minister Binyamin Netanyahu after he insists on talking to Palestinians during a visit to a disputed settlement in east Jerusalem.

Old Trafford, 18
Manchester United are knocked out of the European Cup after drawing 1-1 at home to Monaco in the second leg of the quarter-finals.

London, 18
Paul Burrel, 39, former butler to Diana, Princess of Wales, is appointed fund-raising manager of her memorial fund.

Southern Ocean, 18
The attempt by yachtswoman Tracey Edwards and her all-female crew to sail non-stop around the world is scuppered when the mast of their catamaran, *Royal & Sun Alliance*, is snapped by a freak wave.

Los Angeles, 19
Media mogul Rupert Murdoch buys the Los Angeles Dodgers baseball team for $350 million through his Fox Group.

DEATHS
March 21. Galina Ulanova, former prima ballerina with Russia's Bolshoi Ballet, dies aged 88.

London, Thursday 19. Up to 8,000 fans crammed into Leicester Square and screamed in vain for a sight of Leonardo DiCaprio at the opening of his latest movie, *The Man in the Iron Mask*, premiered at the Odeon cinema today. Concerned police smuggled him in through a side entrance.

NIGERIA, SATURDAY 21

Pope calls on Nigerian ruler to respect human rights

Pope John Paul II and Nigerian president Sani Abacha wave to the crowds in Abuja.

Pope John Paul II today began a visit to Nigeria, Africa's most populous country. Many Nigerians are hoping that his presence will strike a blow against the country's military ruler, General Sani Abacha.

General Abacha seized power in 1993 and annulled the result of democratic elections. The Abacha regime was widely condemned in 1995 for the execution of writer Ken Saro-Wiwa.

Standing alongside the general on arrival in the Nigerian capital, Abuja, Pope John Paul called for "efforts to foster harmony and guarantee respect for human rights". He later handed General Abacha a list of 60 political prisoners whom the Vatican would like to see released.

TYNESIDE, MONDAY 16

Newcastle directors outrage Geordie "dogs"

There have been calls for the resignation of two directors of Newcastle United football club after the *News of the World* alleged that the two men had described the women of Newcastle as "dogs".

Club chairman Freddie Shepherd and majority shareholder Douglas Hall also allegedly boasted of their sexual exploits, mocked fans for buying overpriced replica shirts, and derided players – dubbing the club's £15 million striker Alan Shearer "Mary Poppins".

Sports Minister Tony Banks told the press today: "If what is claimed was said was actually said, the views are distasteful and quite frankly will anger all decent fans."

The Newcastle United board has not yet officially commented on the newspaper allegations. The club's share price fell sharply today on the stock exchange. (→ March 23)

Chancellor delivers a "family-friendly" Budget

The Chancellor of the Exchequer, Gordon Brown, pulled off a political coup with his first full Budget presented to the House of Commons today. He managed to allay middle-class fears about savings and taxes, but at the same time respond to charges that New Labour was uncaring towards poorer families.

Declaring his goal to "make work pay", the Chancellor promised all families with one member in full-time work a minimum weekly income of £180. Other "family-friendly" measures included subsidies to help working mothers afford childcare and a rise in child benefit.

To please the better-off, the Chancellor abandoned the £50,000 upper limit on tax-free savings proposed by the Government last year. He also promised to maintain strict controls on government spending.

In a pre-Budget photo-call, Gordon Brown and girlfriend Sarah Macauley celebrate the birthday of Ben, son of his political secretary, Sue Nye.

Parenting guru Dr Spock dies

Spock countered rigid theories of childcare.

Dr Benjamin Spock, the man whose views on childcare revolutionized attitudes to parenting, has died in San Diego, California, aged 94.

His book *Baby and Child Care*, published in 1946, told parents to hug their children and follow their instincts, rather than imposing set routines and rigorous discipline. In the 1960s he was a prominent opponent of America's war in Vietnam.

Britain, Thursday 19. Lieutenant Sue Moore takes command of *HMS Dasher* at Portsmouth. Moore and Lieutenant Melanie Rees, who joined *HMS Express* in Ayrshire, are the first women to command warships in the 400-year history of the Royal Navy.

Clinton faces renewed sex allegations

President Bill Clinton, already on the defensive over the Paula Jones case and allegations about his relations with Monica Lewinsky, was today hit by another embarrassing tale of sexual harassment.

Interviewed on CBS's prime-time television news show *60 Minutes,* former White House volunteer Kathleen Willey described in graphic detail an alleged encounter with the president in November 1993. She claims that the president made a pass at her in the Oval Office at the White House. He allegedly touched her breasts and placed her hand on his genitals. She claims that she then pushed him away and walked out.

Clinton has already responded to these allegations, which were first deposed with lawyers in January. He says that Ms Willey was upset that day and that he put his arms round her to comfort her. "There was nothing sexual about it," the president said. Whether the American people will accept his version of events remains to be seen. (→ April 1)

S	M	T	W	T	F	S
1	2	3	4	5	6	7
8	9	10	11	12	13	14
15	16	17	18	19	20	21
22	23	24	25	26	27	28
29	30	31				

Northern Ireland, 23
The Northern Ireland peace talks resume with the participation of Sinn Fein after a two-week ban. (→ April 10)

Newcastle, 23
Newcastle United directors Freddie Shepherd and Douglas Hall resign in the wake of the scandal caused by their alleged derogatory comments on the club's fans and Geordie women.

Moscow, 23
Russian President Boris Yeltsin sacks the government of Viktor Chernomyrdin and appoints unknown 35-year-old Sergei Kiriyenko as acting prime minister. (→ May 28)

London, 25
The public inquiry into the 1993 murder of black youth Stephen Lawrence opens. The inquiry had been delayed after the Lawrence family expressed doubts about the racial attitudes of the chairman, Sir William Macpherson. (→ May 13)

Gillingham, 28
Fighting breaks out between gangs of rival fans after a football match between Gillingham and Fulham, and a Fulham supporter, Matthew Fox, is murdered.

Wembley, 29
Under the new management of Gianluca Vialli, Chelsea win the Coca-Cola Cup, beating Middlesbrough 2-0 in extra time.

São Paulo, 29
Finnish driver Mika Hakkinen wins the Brazilian Grand Prix, opening up a clear lead in the Formula One drivers' championship. (→ April 12)

Somerset, 30
Pop star Gary Glitter is charged with possessing indecent pictures of children on his computer. The singer's solicitor says: "Gary will be vigorously contesting these allegations".

City of London, 30
On international exchanges, sterling reaches its highest level for a decade. The value of the pound has risen by about a third in the last two years.

DEATHS
March 27. Ferdinand Porsche, German car manufacturer, dies in Zell-am-See, Austria, aged 88.

March 27. Joan Lestor, Baroness Lestor of Eccles, Labour politician and women's rights campaigner, dies aged 66.

Blockbuster *Titanic* sweeps record 11 Academy Awards

A still from the hit film Titanic *showing a lifeboat being lowered into the freezing sea.*

Nominees: British actresses Kate Winslet (left) and Helena Bonham Carter.

This year's Oscars were dominated by *Titanic*, the most expensive movie ever made. It took 11 Academy Awards, including best picture and best director for James Cameron, equalling the record held by *Ben Hur*.

It was a disappointing night for Britain. The four British stars nominated for best actress were all pipped by American Helen Hunt, honoured for her role in *As Good As It Gets*. Low-budget British success *The Full Monty*, with four nominations, won one Oscar, for best original music.

Titanic star Leonardo DiCaprio was an absentee from the Oscar ceremony, having failed to win a nomination. Jack Nicholson won best actor, also for *As Good As It Gets*.

Pilot saves Leeds football team from crash tragedy

The Emerald Airways jet crash-landed at Stansted with the Leeds football team on board.

Quick-thinking pilot Captain John Hackett averted an air disaster this evening when he safely crash-landed his aircraft taking off from Stansted airport. On board were the Leeds United football team, returning to the North after a match against east London side West Ham.

As the propeller-driven Emerald Airways BAe 748 lifted off from the ground, one of the engines exploded. The 61-year-old pilot immediately aborted the flight and the plane came to a halt nose-down just beyond the runway. The 40 passengers escaped through emergency exits as fire crews dowsed the flames.

ANTIGUA, TUESDAY 24

Atherton bows out after England lose in Windies

Michael Atherton resigned today as captain of the England cricket side, only minutes after losing the last Test of the current series against the West Indies. The shattering defeat, by an innings and 52 runs, gave the home side a 3-1 victory in the Test series.

Atherton had been England captain since 1993, leading the team in a record 52 Test matches. "A combination of our failure to win this series and my own form," he said, "has led me to believe that it is time for someone else to lead the side."

Atherton, who celebrated his 30th birthday yesterday, is likely to be succeeded by his fellow opening batsman Alec Stewart. (→ May 5)

ARKANSAS, WEDNESDAY 25

Schoolyard massacre shocks America

Andrew Golden, arrested for the Jonesboro killings, seen in a home video when he was six.

Two children, Mitchell Johnson, 13, and Andrew Golden, 11, appeared in an Arkansas court today charged with killing four girls and a teacher in a gun massacre at their school.

The killings took place at around 12.40 p.m. yesterday. The two boys approached Westside Middle School, Jonesboro, dressed in camouflage gear and armed with an array of rifles and pistols. They fired on pupils and teachers as they evacuated the school building in response to a fire alarm.

The four girls killed were all aged 11 and 12. Teacher Shannon Wright died after using her body to shield another child from the gunfire.

Mitchell Johnson had reportedly been jilted by his girlfriend and was bent on revenge. He told friends: "I've got a lot of killing to do."

CANADA, WEDNESDAY 25

Prince William delights Vancouver

Prince William shows off his "street cred" to his father Charles, donning a Canadian baseball jacket and "poor boy" cap he was given.

Prince Charles and his sons, Prince William and Prince Harry, arrived in Canada yesterday for what was meant to be a private skiing holiday. But the visit has turned into a very public display of William's new status as an adolescent heart-throb.

The 15-year-old prince was greeted by a crowd of screaming teenage girls when he arrived at Vancouver airport. Today, visiting a high school with his father and brother, he delighted the audience with a display of cool, donning a "poor boy" cap fashionably back-to-front and posing with a shoulder-shrugging rap-artist style body language.

William is even more popular in America than in Britain. One young Canadian girl called him "the British version of Leonardo DiCaprio".

MIAMI, THURSDAY 26

Brain-damaged Nikki speaks after dolphin therapy

An eight-year-old boy who had been mute from birth has spoken for the first time after swimming with dolphins at a Florida aquarium.

Nikki Brice, from Weston-super-Mare, Somerset, was enrolled at the Miami centre after failing to respond to other treatments. He received speech therapy, rewarded by sessions playing with dolphins in the pool. Within days, he said his first word.

Nikki's mother, Tabitha Brice, said: "There is just something magical that happens between children and dolphins, something that I don't think we will ever fully understand."

Nikki Brice swimming with dolphins at the Sea Aquarium in Miami, Florida.

S	M	T	W	T	F	S
			1	2	3	4
5	6	7	8	9	10	11
12	13	14	15	16	17	18
19	20	21	22	23	24	25
26	27	28	29	30		

Wayland Prison, Norfolk, 1
The East End gangster Reggie Kray is denied parole after serving 30 years for the murder of Jack "the Hat" McVitie. A medical report notes that Kray "conveyed feelings of suppressed aggression".

Bristol, 2
Miles Evans, the soldier stepfather of nine-year-old Zoe Evans, who was murdered last year, is given a life sentence for the killing.

London, 3
Police are investigating claims that love letters written by Princess Diana were stolen from her former lover James Hewitt. A newspaper claims that they had bought them from a spurned lover of Hewitt's, but agreed not to publish them.

London, 3
Sculptor Anthony-Noel Kelly is sentenced at Southwark crown court to nine months in prison for stealing body parts from the Royal College of Surgeons.

Aintree, 4
Earth Summit wins the Grand National, watched by an estimated 500 million people in more than 60 countries. Only six of the 37 horses finished the race, however, and three were killed.

London, 4
Arsenal striker Dennis Bergkamp is voted Player of the Year by the Professional Footballers' Association; Michael Owen is voted Young Player of the Year.

Wembley, London, 4
France defeat Wales 51-0 to record their biggest-ever Five Nations rugby union victory. It completes a notable Grand Slam for France in the tournament.

Washington, D.C., 6
Researchers at the US National Cancer Institute claim that women at high risk of breast cancer might be able to halve their chances of contracting the disease by taking the drug tamoxifen.

Plymouth, 11
Comedian and actor Rik Mayall is in a coma after a quad bike accident at his home in south Devon.

DEATHS
April 6. Tammy Wynette, dubbed the "first lady of country music", dies from a blood clot at the age of 55.

April 11. Francis Durbridge, prolific author of thrillers, dies aged 85.

BRITAIN, THURSDAY 9
Worst floods to hit central England this century

Fire-fighters battle against the floods in the Warwickshire town of Leamington Spa.

Heavy rain swept across the English Midlands today, causing widespread floods and traffic chaos. Railways were severely disrupted, while traffic on a 65-km (40-mile) stretch of the M40 motorway was brought to a complete standstill. After closing the M40 at Junction 8, a police spokesman said: "The motorway is flooded and closed because we believe the tarmac is lifting."

The worst hit areas include the Severn and Thames valleys and East Anglia. In Northampton, a woman was swept from a barge into the River Nene. The Environment Agency confirmed that the floods were the worst in living memory, with a month's rainfall falling in just 24 hours on the River Avon at Evesham in Worcestershire.

TOKYO, THURSDAY 2
Japan's economy near collapse

Japan may face economic disaster, according to an influential business survey published by the Bank of Japan. The mood of gloom was further darkened by comments from the president of Sony, Norio Ohga, who said: "The Japanese economy is on the verge of collapsing." He called on the Japanese government to stimulate consumer demand. A sharp downturn in Japan, the second-largest economy in the world, would send shock waves across the globe.

LONDON, THURSDAY 2
Rally driver is found guilty of road rage deaths

Jason Humble, a rally driver with 24 previous traffic convictions, was sentenced to 12 years' imprisonment today for the manslaughter of Toby Exley and Karen Martin last October. Humble killed the couple by repeatedly ramming their Ford Fiesta with his own car in a fit of road rage. The Fiesta then crashed through a barrier into oncoming traffic; both occupants died instantly from multiple injuries.

LOS ANGELES, WEDNESDAY 8
Singer George Michael arrested for "lewd behaviour" in lavatory

Singer George Michael was released on bail after his arrest in Beverly Hills.

British pop singer George Michael was charged today with performing a "lewd act" in front of an undercover police officer. The singer was arrested yesterday in a men's lavatory in a Beverly Hills park. After being booked, he was released on $500 bail.

Michael achieved fame as part of the pop duo Wham! before embarking on a solo career. Although refusing to talk about his sex life, he admitted loving Anselmo Feleppa, a Brazilian who died of an Aids-related brain haemorrhage in 1993. (→ May 14)

NORTHERN IRELAND, FRIDAY 10

Peace breakthrough on Good Friday

Tony Blair with US peacebroker George Mitchell (centre) and Irish prime minister Bertie Ahern at the negotiations.

Late on this Good Friday evening, the political parties sitting around the negotiating table finally agreed to a peace settlement for Northern Ireland. The agreement has brought the bitterly opposed Unionist and nationalist parties together for the first time – offering hope to an end to 30 years of bloodshed.

Central to the agreement is the formation of an elected Northern Ireland assembly, a power-sharing executive committee, and new institutions linking the North with the Republic. Also under discussion is the release of prisoners from both sides, a promise to begin decommissioning of arms, and reform of the Royal Ulster Constabulary.

Both Bertie Ahern, the Irish prime minister, and British premier Tony Blair played crucial roles in keeping the talks going in the final 33-hour session which led up to the agreement. Blair hailed the accord as a triumph of courage: "I said when I arrived here on Wednesday night that I felt the hand of history upon us. Today, I hope that the burden of history can at long last be lifted from our shoulders." (→ April 18)

Sinn Fein's Gerry Adams (right) and Martin McGuinness hail the historic agreement.

ARKANSAS, WEDNESDAY 1

Judge throws out Paula Jones case

An Arkansas judge has rejected Paula Jones's sexual harassment lawsuit against President Bill Clinton. Judge Susan Webber Wright dismissed all the charges, ruling them unworthy of trial. Jones had claimed that Clinton unzipped himself in a hotel room and demanded oral sex. White House sources said the President was "thrilled" at the ruling. (→ June 30)

East End, Friday 10. It's true, Cath really is leaving Albert Square. In a tear-jerking episode of *EastEnders*, actress Gillian Taylforth packs her bags and heads off to South Africa.

KENT, THURSDAY 9

Robin cooks up quiet wedding

Foreign Secretary Robin Cook gave Fleet Street the slip today when he discreetly married his fiancée, Gaynor Regan, at a registry office in Tunbridge Wells, Kent. The newly married couple then proceeded to a wedding party at Chevening, the official residence of the foreign secretary. Mr Cook made it known that he would be paying for the food and drink out of his own purse.

S	M	T	W	T	F	S
			1	2	3	4
5	6	7	8	9	10	11
12	13	14	15	16	17	18
19	20	21	22	23	24	25
26	27	28	29	30		

Argentina, 12
Michael Schumacher wins the Argentinian Grand Prix. David Coulthard later criticizes the German's driving tactics as being "outside the spirit and rules of Formula One". (→ April 26)

Northern Ireland, 18
Ulster Unionist leader David Trimble persuades his party to back the Northern Ireland peace agreement. (→ May 10)

Manchester, 18
Featherweight Prince Naseem retains his world title, stopping Wilfredo Vazquez of Puerto Rico in the seventh round of their bout. Chris Eubank loses to cruiserweight Carl Thompson on points.

New York, 21
The *New York Post* announces that media mogul Rupert Murdoch and his wife Anna are to divorce.

Westminster, 21
Prime Minister Tony Blair admits that a cache of weapons-grade nuclear waste from the ex-Soviet republic of Georgia is to be brought to the nuclear plant at Dounreay, Scotland, for reprocessing.

Selkirk, 21
A Scottish court throws out the case against hotelier Jim Sutherland, who was prosecuted under new government regulations after serving beef on the bone to guests at his hotel in February.

Paris, 22
Tickets for the football World Cup finals go on sale. Over 20 million people phone the hotline on the first day, but only 15,000 manage to buy tickets.

Wembley, 22
Alan Shearer scores two goals as England beat Portugal 3-0 in a World Cup warm-up match. (→ April 30)

DEATHS
April 13. Sir Ian MacGregor, Scottish businessman who was chairman of the National Coal Board during the miners' strike of 1984-85, dies aged 85.

April 14. Dorothy Squires, the 1950s cabaret singer and the first wife of movie actor Roger Moore, dies aged 83.

April 20. Archbishop Trevor Huddleston, a founder of the Anti-Apartheid Movement, dies aged 84.

April 23. James Earl Ray, killer of civil rights leader Martin Luther King in 1968, dies in prison aged 70.

LONDON, SUNDAY 19
Attack on Diana outrages Blair

Professor Anthony O'Hear, a lecturer in philosophy, has made a swingeing attack on the reputation of Diana, Princess of Wales. In a book published last week, he says she was self-obsessed and childlike, and calls the reaction to her death "mob grief".

Prime Minister Tony Blair, an avid admirer of Diana, responded today by accusing her critics of "snobbery" and "insulting people's feelings".

CANTERBURY, SUNDAY 12
Gays halt Carey's Easter sermon

Gay rights activist Peter Tatchell disrupted a packed Easter service in Canterbury Cathedral today. As the Archbishop of Canterbury began his sermon, Tatchell and other protesters clambered into the pulpit, holding banners accusing Dr Carey of bias against homosexuals. Tatchell was charged with "riotous and violent behaviour in a church". (→ August 5)

CALIFORNIA, FRIDAY 17
Linda McCartney loses fight against cancer

Sir Paul and Linda on their wedding day. They only ever spent one night apart.

Linda McCartney lost her three-year fight against cancer tonight in Santa Barbara, aged 56. Her husband Sir Paul, their three children, Mary, Stella, and James, and Linda's daughter Heather, were with her when she died. Linda built up a multi-million pound food business around her profound belief in vegetarianism, and Sir Paul has asked that mourners should make "the tribute that Linda would like best: Go veggie". (→ June 8)

London, Sunday 19. At the Bafta awards, fellow Scot Billy Connolly presents actor Sean Connery with a lifetime achievement award for his contribution to film. Other home-grown winners on the night included Judi Dench for her role in *Mrs Brown*, and Robert Carlyle for the surprise hit, *The Full Monty*.

AUGUSTA, SUNDAY 12
Unfancied veteran wins US Masters

This year's US Masters golf tournament has been a triumph for the veterans of the professional circuit. Jack Nicklaus, who won his first major trophy in 1962, tied for sixth place at the age of 58. Gary Player, aged 62, became the oldest man to complete all four rounds. And the shock winner was 41-year-old Mark O'Meara, a respected but modest golfer who had never won a major tournament and was considered too old to start doing so now.

Golfer Mark O'Meara celebrates the putt that won him the coveted Green Jacket.

BISHAM ABBEY, MONDAY 20
Hoddle defends use of faith healer

England soccer coach Glenn Hoddle today confronted the press over his use of a faith healer, Eileen Drewery, to treat his injury-hit squad in the run-up to the World Cup finals.

Drewery is now lodged at the England team hotel. The England manager claimed that three-quarters of his players had been to see her at some time, with fruitful results.

Hoddle's strong religious beliefs are well known, He told sceptical journalists: "Keep your minds open. Go and see her yourself."

CAMBODIA, THURSDAY 16
Despot Pol Pot's body put on show

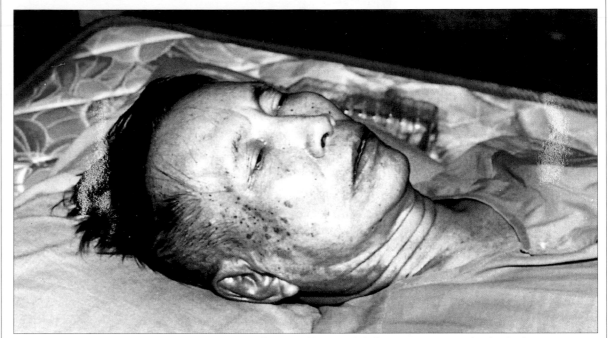

The body of brutal Khmer Rouge leader Pol Pot is shown off to the world's press while the controversy surrounding his death grows.

Pol Pot, former leader of Cambodia's tyrannical communist Khmer Rouge regime, has died in an isolated village in the north of the country. The timing of his death is, to say the least, expedient. It is rumoured that the present Khmer Rouge leader, Ta Mok, may have had him killed rather than allow him to face a trial in which Khmer Rouge links with the present Cambodian regime might have been exposed. Pol Pot's communist party ruled over Cambodia between 1975-79 and was responsible for the deaths of up to 1.7 million people by execution or starvation in the infamous "killing fields". After his downfall, he disappeared in the hills of northern Cambodia and was not seen in public for 18 years. In death, as in life, he has eluded justice.

MANCHESTER, THURSDAY 16
"Weatherfield One" is freed after PM intervenes

Coronation Street fans fighting the "Free Deirdre" campaign. Even the PM backed them.

Following intervention at the very highest level, Deirdre Rachid, the "Weatherfield One", has walked free from jail pending an appeal against her sentence. The fictional character in *Coronation Street*, played by actress Anne Kirkbride, had, in the nation's eyes, been wrongly imprisoned, while her adulterous boyfriend escaped with a suspended sentence for fraud.

In a strange blurring of fact and fantasy, the public mounted a noisy campaign to protest Mrs Rachid's innocence. Even Tony Blair joined in the fun, backing Fraser Kemp, MP for Houghton and Washington East, in appealing to the Home Secretary, Jack Straw, on Ms Rachid's behalf. Tory leader William Hague also leapt on the bandwagon, hinting that Deirdre was "taken in by a sharp, smooth-talking con-artist" in much the same way as the British electorate.

S	M	T	W	T	F	S
					1	2
3	4	5	6	7	8	9
10	11	12	13	14	15	16
17	18	19	20	21	22	23
24	25	26	27	28	29	30
31						

Britain, 2
It is revealed that murderer Mary Bell received £15,000, and not £50,000 as was claimed last week, for collaborating with author Gitta Sereny in the writing of a book about her life.

Highbury, 3
Arsenal clinch the FA Premiership with a 4-0 victory over Everton. It gives them a seven point lead over Manchester United with two games to play. (→ May 17)

London, 3
Boxer Spencer Oliver undergoes an operation to remove a blood clot from his brain after being knocked out by Ukrainian Sergei Devakov in a bout at the Albert Hall yesterday.

Vatican, 4
Alois Estermann, newly appointed commander of the Papal Swiss Guard, is shot in a triple killing. His wife and fellow Swiss Guard Cedric Tornay also die.

Sheffield, 4
Scottish player John Higgins beats Ken Doherty 18-12 in the final of snooker's Embassy World Championship.

Montana, 4
Former professor Theodore Kaczynski, nicknamed the Unabomber, is given four life sentences for his 17-year reign of terror in the United States. He killed three people and injured more than 20 in a series of bomb attacks.

Lord's, 5
Wicketkeeper Alec Stewart is appointed to captain the England cricket team for this summer's Test series against South Africa and Sri Lanka.

Twickenham, 9
In an all-London rugby union final, Saracens trounce Wasps 48-18 to win the Tetley's Bitter Cup.

Celtic Park, 9
Celtic win the Scottish Premiership with a 2-0 home win over St Johnstone, ending the nine-year reign of Rangers.

DEATHS
May 1. Eldridge Cleaver, American black radical, a Black Panther leader in the 1960s, and author of the best-selling *Soul on Ice*, dies aged 62.

May 5. Syd Lawrence, big band leader, dies aged 74.

BRUSSELS, SUNDAY 3
Euro launch on target after Brussels fudge

After 11 hours of frantic negotiations between European leaders, a deal was hammered out in the early hours of this morning that will allow the single European currency to be introduced on schedule in 1999.

The question that threatened to derail the whole process was the identity of the head of the new European Central Bank (ECB), meant to be appointed for an eight-year term. Germany was backing the Dutch candidate, Wim Duisenberg, but France was implacably opposed.

The heated debate was chaired by Tony Blair, as Britain currently holds the presidency of the European Union. Eventually, Duisenberg was confirmed as the first head of the ECB, but only on condition that he agreed to retire after four years, when a Frenchman would take over.

British Tory leader William Hague reacted angrily to what he called "a fistful of fudges". But German Chancellor Helmut Kohl said simply: "It's done. The Euro is here."

ITALY, WEDNESDAY 6
Mudslides devastate Italian towns

An angel rises above the mud that swept through Sarno, where at least 18 people died.

After torrential rainfall, a series of mudslides have struck hillside towns in Italy between Salerno and Naples. More than 100 people have died. In the worst-hit town of Sarno, "a sea of mud poured down like lava," according to one witness. Buildings and people were swept away.

The mudslides are being blamed on illegal building work. One Italian newspaper said the smell of the mud was really "the stench of corruption".

BIRMINGHAM, SATURDAY 9
Israeli transsexual wins Eurovision Song Contest

Dana International is one of Israel's most controversial stars and provokes a mixed reaction.

Dana International tonight became the first Israeli singer to win the Eurovision Song Contest. Her song *Diva* narrowly beat the Maltese entry.

The victory for Dana was far from being universally welcomed by the Israelis, however, because she is a transsexual. Born Yaron Cohen, she had a sex-change operation in 1993.

Ultra-Orthodox Jews in Israel, who are campaigning to enforce a strict religious-based morality in the country, were furious when Dana was chosen to represent Israel in the competition. They are even more unhappy now that she has won, and have vowed to disrupt the song contest if, according to the rules, it is held in Israel next year. Rabbi Haim Miller said: "Such a shameful event will not take place in Jerusalem."

A triumphant Dana claimed the victory as a blow against prejudice. She said: "I did it for us to live freely in the world without hate."

Sad demise of former football star

Justin Fashanu, the former Norwich and Nottingham Forest striker, has committed suicide. His body was found yesterday in a garage under a railway arch in east London.

Fashanu, who was a homosexual, had recently fled to England from the United States, where he was facing an allegation of sexual assault lodged by a 17-year-old boy. He vehemently denied the allegation.

As children, Justin and his brother John, also a footballer, were sent to a Dr Barnardo's home. They were adopted by a white family in a small Norfolk village. Justin made his reputation in the late 1970s as one of England's most promising young footballers. In 1981 he was signed by

Nottingham Forest manager Brian Clough for £1 million, but his goalscoring touch soon deserted him.

The revelation of his gay sexual orientation caused uproar in the strongly homophobic world of football. His career was already on a downward spiral when injury forced him out of the game.

Justin became estranged from his brother. They had not spoken for seven years. John Fashanu's solicitor today issued a statement saying: "John is truly shocked and distressed by the news of his brother's death. Although there were periods of disagreement between them, there were also many occasions when they enjoyed special times together." (→ September 9)

From glory to tragedy: Justin Fashanu

"Bill" star drinks himself into the grave

Kevin Lloyd, the actor known to millions for his role as Tosh Lines in ITV's police soap *The Bill*, has died after a drinking binge. He was 49.

Lloyd had been sacked from his part in the TV series earlier in the week, apparently after arriving on set drunk and having difficulty saying his lines. He subsequently enrolled at a rehabilitation clinic in the village of Rolleston on Dove, Staffordshire. He continued to drink, however, and collapsed this afternoon.

Billy Murray, a fellow actor in *The Bill*, said "Everybody loved Kevin. People are just shocked and sad."

In better times: Kevin with his family.

Londoners back elected mayor

In a referendum held yesterday, London voters approved the New Labour plan for an elected mayor and assembly to run the city's affairs.

The proposal was backed by almost four out of five of those who bothered to vote — but in fact only one Londoner in three actually turned up at the polling booths.

Apathy was also the main winner in local elections held in England's towns and cities on the same day. Overall, turnout was under 30 per cent, but the Tories took some comfort from better results than expected.

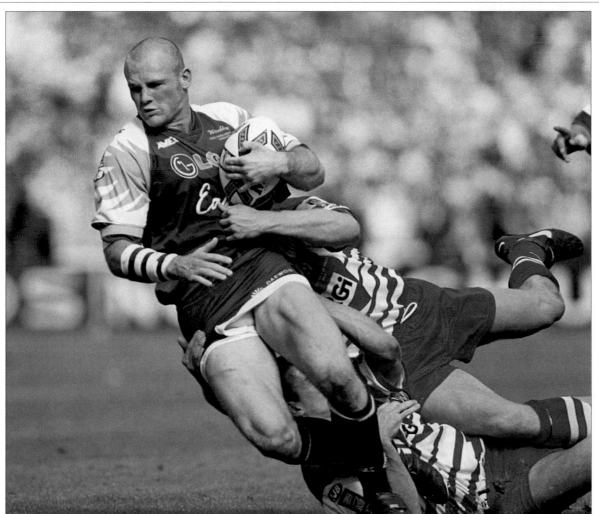

Wembley, Saturday 2. Keith Senior of the Sheffield Eagles surges forward during his side's sensational 17-8 victory over the Wigan Warriors in the final of the rugby Challenge Cup. It was the first time the Eagles, set up 13 years ago, had won a major trophy; Wigan have won the Challenge Cup 16 times.

S	M	T	W	T	F	S
					1	2
3	4	5	6	7	8	9
10	11	12	13	14	15	16
17	18	19	20	21	22	23
24	25	26	27	28	29	30
31						

Dublin, 10
At a party conference, Sinn Fein votes to accept the Good Friday peace agreement and participate in a future Northern Ireland assembly. (→ May 23)

Barcelona, 10
Mika Hakkinen wins the Spanish Grand Prix. His McLaren team colleague, David Coulthard, is second. (→ May 24)

Britain, 11
Official figures show that train services on many routes are less punctual than they were before the railways were privatized in 1997.

Hillsborough, 12
An FA inquiry finds England captain Alan Shearer not guilty of "an alleged breach of the rules". Shearer had been accused of kicking Leicester City player Neil Lennon in the face on 29 April.

Stockholm, 13
Chelsea win the European Cup Winners' Cup, beating VfB Stuttgart 1-0 thanks to a goal from substitute Gianfranco Zola.

London, 13
At the inquiry into the murder of Stephen Lawrence, Detective Superintendent Ian Crampton admits making a serious mistake by failing to arrest key suspects quickly after the killing. (→ May 27)

Los Angeles, 14
Singer George Michael is sentenced to 80 days' community service for lewd conduct. He was arrested in a Beverly Hills lavatory in April.

Britain, 21
Nurses Lucille McLauchlan and Deborah Parry arrive back in the country after being released from prison in Saudi Arabia. They were jailed last year by a Saudi court following the murder of Australian nurse Yvonne Gilford.

London, 21
Former cabinet minister Jonathan Aitken is charged with perjury and conspiracy to pervert the course of justice. The charges concern his failed libel case against *The Guardian* newspaper last year.

DEATHS
May 17. Hugh Cudlipp, Lord Cudlipp of Aldingbourne, journalist who made the *Daily Mirror* Britain's leading tabloid after World War II, dies aged 84.

Cook embroiled in Sandline African arms affair

Over the past week Robin Cook, the foreign secretary, has found himself at the centre of a confused whirlwind of media allegations concerning the part played by a private company, Sandline International, in a breach of a UN arms embargo.

Sandline has claimed that it had the backing of the Foreign Office for support it gave to the overthrow of a military junta in Sierra Leone in March. The UN had placed a ban on all arms supplies to the conflict zone.

Robin Cook has denied that he knew of the Sandline operation. This stance puzzles many Sierra Leoneans, who wonder why Britain does not take pride in helping to restore democracy in their country. Meanwhile, Prime Minister Tony Blair has tried to calm the media storm by dismissing the affair as just a "hoo-ha".

Madrid, Tuesday 12. In a brief ceremony at the Las Ventas bullring today, Spanish matador Cristina Sanchez became the first woman admitted to the highest rank of bullfighters.

Ulster votes for peace after hard-fought campaign

Bono of Irish band U2 is flanked by Unionist leader David Trimble (left) and SDLP leader John Hume at a concert held in Belfast two days before the referendum.

In a referendum on the future of Northern Ireland held yesterday, voters on both sides of the Irish border have overwhelmingly backed the Good Friday peace agreement.

The final count shows 71 per cent in favour in Northern Ireland and 94 per cent in the Irish Republic.

There will now be elections for an all-party assembly in Ulster.

Northern Ireland Secretary Mo Mowlam described the referendum result as "a resounding victory for the people of Northern Ireland". She said: "They have voted to take the gun out of politics." (→ June 27)

Fans mourn the death of Ol' Blue Eyes

Singer and actor Frank Sinatra died today at the Cedars Sinai Medical Center in Beverly Hills at the age of 82. He leaves a fortune believed to total around $200 million.

Sinatra was the only son of Italian immigrants living in Hoboken, New Jersey. He made his name singing with the big bands of the 1940s. The first "teen idol", he was mobbed by screaming bobby-soxers. In the 1950s and 1960s, he adapted his singing style to appeal to a more mature audience. He also developed a screen career, winning an Oscar for his role in the epic *From Here To Eternity*.

Sinatra had a complex, often stormy, private life and married four times. His ex-wives include actresses Ava Gardner and Mia Farrow. Sinatra is survived by Barbara, his last wife.

Legendary crooner Frank Sinatra.

LONDON, SUNDAY 17

Arsenal double Dutch triumph

An estimated 200,000 Arsenal fans lined the streets of north London today to celebrate a double victory in the league and cup.

Already the winners of the FA Carling Premiership, Arsenal beat Newcastle United 2-0 in the FA Cup final at Wembley yesterday. Typically for a season that had seen a massive influx of foreigners into the English game, Arsenal were led to victory by a French manager, Arsene Wenger, and the stars of their season included Dutch duo Marc Overmars and Denis Bergkamp.

Arsenal last achieved the double in 1971. They are only the second club to manage the feat twice.

Dutchmen Marc Overmars (left) and Denis Bergkamp display the Premiership and FA Cup trophies on the balcony of Islington town hall.

LONDON, MONDAY 18

Gazza grilled over kebab incident

Under the banner headline "Pittaful", yesterday's *Mirror* newspaper carried a picture of England footballer Paul Gascoigne tucking into a kebab. This was the hook for an attack on the player's attitude to his preparation for next month's World Cup finals. He reportedly had two nights out on the town last week with rock star Rod Stewart and DJ Chris Evans.

Despite worries about his fitness, Gazza is in the 30-man England squad which will play warm-up games before the World Cup. He claimed in a recent interview to be "totally one-minded about England", but speculation is mounting that he may not make the 22-man squad for the finals themselves. (→ May 29)

Birmingham, Friday 15. President Bill Clinton, in Birmingham for the G8 summit, drops in for a pint of bitter and a plate of chips at a canal-side pub. He chats with local couple Bill and June Scott.

JAKARTA, WEDNESDAY 20

Suharto steps down as Indonesians riot

President Suharto of Indonesia today resigned after more than 30 years as leader of one of the world's most populous nations. His resignation followed weeks of civil unrest in which thousands have died.

Opposition groups had planned a million-strong march in the capital, Jakarta, today, but were deterred by a clear threat from the Indonesian army of a massacre if they went ahead. Military leaders clearly hope that Suharto's resignation will calm protests. He is succeeded by his deputy, Jusuf Habibie, who promised an end to corruption and nepotism.

Suharto has been forced out of office.

LONDON, THURSDAY 21

Single mother wins Tube job fight

Susan Edwards, a single parent who was told that she had a choice between being "a train driver or a mum", today won a sex discrimination case in the Court of Appeal.

The court ruled that a shift system introduced by London Underground in 1992 discriminated against women by making it impossible to combine childcare with work. Ms Edwards was forced to quit her job as a driver when the new shifts came in.

S	M	T	W	T	F	S
					1	2
3	4	5	6	7	8	9
10	11	12	13	14	15	16
17	18	19	20	21	22	23
24	25	26	27	28	29	30
31						

Cannes, 24
Scottish actor Paul Mullan wins the best actor award at the Cannes Film Festival for his moving portrayal of an alcoholic in the British film *My Name is Joe*, directed by Ken Loach.

Monte Carlo, 24
McLaren driver Mika Hakkinen wins the Monaco Grand Prix, his fourth Formula One victory this season. (→ June 7)

Wembley, 25
Following a gripping 4–4 draw after extra time, Charlton defeat Sunderland 7–6 on penalties in the First Division play-offs to decide who will go up to the Premiership in the coming season.

Hong Kong, 25
In elections to the former British colony's Legislative Council, pro-democracy parties gain 21 out of 60 seats.

New Jersey, 26
Andy Goram, the Rangers and Scottish goalkeeper, quits Scotland's World Cup training camp and announces his retirement from international football. He says recent allegations about his private life have unsettled him.

Nepal, 27
Tom Whittaker is the first physically disabled man to climb Everest. It was the third attempt by the one-legged Welshman to conquer the mountain.

London, 27
Detective Superintendent Brian Weeden, the policeman leading the Stephen Lawrence murder inquiry, admits he failed to arrest key suspects because of his ignorance of criminal law. (→ June 17)

Scotland, 28
It is revealed that a 15-year-old schoolgirl has been earning pocket money by operating heart-monitoring machines attached to dangerously ill patients at Perth Royal Infirmary.

Moscow, 28
The total collapse of the Russian rouble is averted by a hint of IMF intervention and a punitive rise in Russian interest rates to 150 per cent. (→ August 13)

DEATHS
May 29. Barry Goldwater, maverick Republican senator and US presidential candidate in 1964, dies aged 89.

BRITAIN, SATURDAY 30

Spice Girls split as Ginger drops out

Lengthy speculation surrounding the possible departure of Ginger Spice, Geri Halliwell, from the Spice Girls was ended today when lawyers met to discuss terms for a separation. Geri had failed to appear with the group in a recent concert in Norway, but the issue had been clouded by rumours that she was suffering from gastroenteritis.

According to insiders, however, Geri had become disillusioned and tired during her years as a Spice Girl, and wants to pursue a solo career.

Giza, Monday 25. The Sphinx is lit up by lasers during a celebration to mark the end of a 10-year restoration project. Traffic pollution in Cairo is a problem for the conservation of Egyptian monuments.

BRISTOL, FRIDAY 29

Surgeons declared incompetent in baby deaths case

The General Medical Council today found three doctors guilty of failing to heed warnings that they were risking babies' lives by continuing to operate on them. In a seven-month inquiry that cost £2.2 million, the GMC investigated 53 operations, in which 29 children died and a further four suffered brain damage.

James Wisheart, a senior surgeon at the Bristol Royal Infirmary, and Janardan Dhasmana, a junior surgeon, continued to carry out heart surgery despite repeated warnings from colleagues that they should stop.

The GMC said that Dr John Roylance, the medical director of the Bristol Healthcare Trust, should have intervened to halt the operations but failed to do so, even though the two surgeons recorded alarmingly high death rates.

The GMC will meet again on 15 June to decide the doctors' fate. Some of the victims' parents do not believe the GMC's investigation has gone far enough. (→ June 18)

Floral tributes stand beside the names of 160 children who allegedly suffered at the hands of incompetent doctors.

ISLAMABAD, THURSDAY 28
Pakistani nuclear explosion is condemned by world leaders

Pakistan today exploded five nuclear devices. The country's president Rafiq Tarar claimed the tests were in direct retaliation for nuclear tests carried out by India earlier this month.

The Pakistan government immediately declared a state of emergency, suspended civil rights, and froze all foreign currency bank accounts in order to prevent a sudden exodus of capital from the country.

US President Bill Clinton had repeatedly pleaded with Pakistan not to go ahead with the tests. "I cannot believe we are about to start the 21st century by having the Indian subcontinent repeat the worst mistakes of the 20th century," Clinton said. Economic sanctions were imposed on Pakistan after news of the blasts reached Washington, D.C., including the cessation of economic aid and the freezing of IMF loans.

Islamic fundamentalist supporters demonstrate in Islamabad in favour of the detonation of the Pakistani nuclear devices.

LONDON, THURSDAY 28
POWs protest at Japanese state visit

Emperor Akihito talks to the Queen at a state banquet held in Buckingham Palace.

As Japan's Emperor Akihito pressed on with a state visit to Britain today, war veterans staged a protest against the failure of the Japanese government to issue an apology for its behaviour toward British prisoners of war during World War II.

The protest took place in central London. As the coach containing the Queen and Akihito passed down the Mall, the veterans lining the route did an abrupt about-face, turning their backs on the Emperor and the Japanese VIPs following the royal coach. Boos and catcalls accompanied the otherwise silent and highly

One of the veterans who protested on the Mall against Emperor Akihito's visit.

disciplined protest. At a banquet held in Buckingham Palace later in the day, the Emperor expressed his regret for the suffering caused to people during the worldwide conflict: "At the thought of the scars of war that they bear, our hearts are filled with deep sorrow and pain."

His sentiments were welcomed by those on the Mall, but they fell short of the full apology demanded by the veterans. In a diplomatic mood, the Queen talked of the suffering caused by the memories of war, but hoped they would act "as a spur to reconciliation" between the two nations.

MOROCCO, FRIDAY 29
Problems for England in World Cup warm-up

Poor performances against Morocco and Belgium have underlined the problems faced by England coach Glenn Hoddle in the run-up to the football World Cup finals. England lost today's match against Belgium on penalties, and an unfit Paul Gascoigne was substituted. One ray of hope was a goal for 18-year-old Michael Owen in Wednesday's 1–0 victory over Morocco. (→ June 1)

BOSTON, WEDNESDAY 27
Lawyer denies attack on client

Elaine Whitfield Sharp, one of Louise Woodward's defence lawyers, has denied saying that she believed the British au pair was guilty of killing Matthew Eappen. After Whitfield Sharp was arrested for drunken driving last Friday, a state trooper claimed that she told him of Woodward's guilt. Whitfield Sharp, however, says the state trooper made the story up. (→ June 1)

June

S	M	T	W	T	F	S
	1	2	3	4	5	6
7	8	9	10	11	12	13
14	15	16	17	18	19	20
21	22	23	24	25	26	27
28	29	30				

Boston, 1
Elaine Whitfield Sharp, one of the lawyers acting for British au pair Louise Woodward, is dismissed from Woodward's defence team after making hostile remarks about her client. (→ June 18)

Cuba, 1
Australian Susie Maroney swims 204 km (128 miles) across the shark-infested Caribbean from Mexico to Cuba. This is a new world record distance for an unassisted ocean swim.

Afghanistan, 1
Reports are filtering through of a major earthquake in a remote area of northern Afghanistan. At least 25 villages are said to have been destroyed.

London, 2
A prize-winning violinist, Hannah Thompson, 25, tells a court that she took part in the smuggling of cocaine worth £500,000 into Britain. She says she did it to pay off debts incurred through drug addiction. (→ June 15)

St Albans, 2
Footballer Vinnie Jones is found guilty on charges of causing actual bodily harm and criminal damage, after an altercation with a neighbour, Timothy Gear, last November. (→ July 2)

Oklahoma, 4
Terry Nichols, convicted of involuntary manslaughter and conspiracy for his part in the Oklahoma City bombing that killed 168 people in 1995, is sentenced to life imprisonment.

Westminster, 5
Donald Dewar, the Scottish Secretary, announces that the Dounreay nuclear plant in northern Scotland is to be progressively closed down.

Ethiopia, 5
The East African states of Ethiopia and Eritrea go to war over disputed territory. Eritrea was part of Ethiopia until five years ago, when it won its independence after a long armed struggle.

Epsom, 6
The Derby is won by High-Rise, ridden by French jockey Olivier Peslier. In an exciting finish, the second-placed horse, City Honours, is beaten by a head.

Brisbane, 6
England's rugby players suffer their worst ever defeat, beaten 76-0 by Australia.

London, Monday 1. An image based on a work by artist Mark Reddy has been chosen as the logo of the Millennium Dome.

CITY OF LONDON, THURS. 4
Bank under fire for interest rate hike

The Bank of England's monetary policy committee came under heavy criticism from trade unions and leading industrialists today for raising the base interest rate a quarter per cent to 7.5 per cent, despite widespread fears of a recession.

It is the sixth time that the Bank has raised interest rates since being handed independent control of base-rate levels after Labour's election victory in May last year. Critics claim that the monetary committee's determination to stamp out inflation may lead to a fall in output and rising unemployment.

High interest rates have led to a rise in the value of the pound, which has made British exports less competitive in world markets. The Bank claims, however, that wage rises remain dangerously high.

HERTFORDSHIRE, MONDAY 1
Controversy rages after Gazza is sent home from the World Cup

A devastated Paul Gascoigne was back in Britain today after being told he had not been selected for the England squad for the World Cup finals starting next week.

Speaking at England's World Cup training ground at La Manga in Spain, manager Glenn Hoddle justified his decision by speaking of Gascoigne's lack of fitness. In an oblique reference to the player's alleged fondness for drinking and late nights, Hoddle said: "He could have done more to help himself."

In an interview with *The Sun*, Gascoigne said: "I was furious and upset when Glenn gave me his decision. And I did go berserk."

The dropping of England's gifted midfielder led to a sharp exchange of views in the House of Commons. The Minister for Sport, Tony Banks, defended the decision as "brave and the right one". (→ October 17)

Dejected Paul Gascoigne leaves the house in the Hertfordshire village of Stanstead Abbots where he spent his first day back in England with his estranged wife, Sheryl.

HAMBURG, WEDNESDAY 3
Carnage as high-speed train hits bridge

Rescue workers hunt for survivors in the wreckage of the German express that crashed into a concrete bridge south of Hamburg.

More than 100 people are believed to have been killed today when a high-speed train travelling from Munich to Hamburg crashed into a bridge near the village of Eschede.

The Inter City Express (ICE) was moving at approximately 125mph (200kmh) when the accident happened. Four of the train's 14 coaches were almost completely destroyed.

Rescue services, aided by local people, struggled to cut survivors from the wreckage. The train was carrying about 400 passengers.

The accident occurred on the same day that the British Government gave the go-ahead to the high-speed rail link between London and the Channel Tunnel. When the link opens in 2003, it will carry trains travelling at up to 180mph (290kmh).

PARIS, FRIDAY 5
Al Fayed makes "snob" jibe

A "witness summit" called by the French magistrate investigating the death of Diana, Princess of Wales, was today attended by Diana's mother, Frances Shand Kydd, and by Mohamed Al Fayed, whose son Dodi also died in the fatal crash.

During a break in the proceedings, Mr Al Fayed launched an astonishing attack on Mrs Shand Kydd, telling journalists she was "a snob" who did not want to talk to "ordinary people" like himself. He also said that she was "not a good mother". The millionaire owner of Harrod's described himself as "just a working-class guy".

SUDAN, WEDNESDAY 3
Short knocks Sudan aid appeal

International Development Secretary Clare Short startled aid agencies by claiming today that an appeal for funds to feed the starving in Sudan was unnecessary. She claimed that the problem was not money but the need to end the civil war. An aid agency spokeswoman replied: "We have got to get aid in to save lives."

BISHAM ABBEY, SATURDAY 6
Sheringham shamed for partying

Teddy Sheringham, a member of England's World Cup squad, had to apologize today for his "lack of professionalism". The *Sun* newspaper had published a photograph of the player in a Portuguese bar, apparently drinking and smoking, taken at 6.45 a.m. last Wednesday.

Sheringham said: "It happened. I can't deny it. I'm just sorry for how it came across." England coach Glenn Hoddle had made it clear that he did not want his players "out drinking". Former England star Sir Bobby Charlton condemned the player's conduct. "I hope that he feels suitably embarrassed," he said.

Dublin, Wednesday 3. Members of the Lynch family from Dublin scored an almost unprecedented musical double today. Shane Lynch (above left) performs with Boyzone, who are top of the albums chart with *Where We Belong*. Edele and Keavy Lynch (above right, left and second left) are members of B*witched, whose *C'est la Vie* currently holds the number one spot in the singles chart.

S	M	T	W	T	F	S
	1	2	3	4	5	6
7	8	9	10	11	12	13
14	15	16	17	18	19	20
21	22	23	24	25	26	27
28	29	30				

London, 7
British Foreign Secretary Robin Cook warns President Milosovic of Yugoslavia not to use "ethnic cleansing" in the province of Kosovo which, although part of Serbia, has a predominantly ethnic Albanian population. (→ October 1)

Paris, 7
Spanish tennis player Carlos Moya, currently seeded No. 12 in the rankings, wins the French Open – his first Grand Slam victory – when he defeats fellow Spaniard Alex Corretja.

New York, 8
British stars triumph at the Tony Awards, with Natasha Richardson and Alan Cumming winning best leading actress and actor for their roles in the musical *Cabaret*, currently showing on Broadway.

London, 9
The ending of the old system of issuing new number plates on August 1 each year is announced. The new system, in which cars will be identified by town and region, will come into force in 2001.

Westminster, 11
Chancellor of the Exchequer Gordon Brown announces a surprise plan to sell off government assets in the British air traffic control system, the Royal Mint, and the horse-racing Tote. The chancellor's intention is to raise up to £12 billion to finance spending on the health service, education, and transport.

Paris, 11
On the basis of posthumous DNA tests, Aurore Drossart loses a paternity suit to establish her claim that the French actor Yves Montand was her father.

Australia, 7
The right-wing One Nation Party led by Pauline Hanson captures more than a quarter of the votes in the Queensland state elections.

DEATHS
June 8. General Sani Abacha, Nigerian dictator, dies suddenly from a suspected heart attack, aged 54.

June 10. Hammond Innes, author of adventure stories, dies aged 84.

June 10. Sir David English, former editor of the *Daily Mail*, dies aged 67.

June 13. Reg Smythe, creator of cartoon character Andy Capp, dies aged 80.

NEWCASTLE, THURSDAY 11
Death of much-loved author Catherine Cookson

Catherine Cookson celebrating her honorary doctorate from Sunderland Polytechnic.

One of the world's most popular authors, Dame Catherine Cookson, died today at her home near Newcastle-upon-Tyne, aged 91. Born into poverty as the illegitimate daughter of an alcoholic mother, she did not start writing until she was 44, yet her books sold more than 100 million copies in 17 languages. Cookson earned an estimated £14 million from her novels, and she was recently listed as the 17th richest woman in Britain.

Cookson's books reflected her own experiences of deprivation and of the individual's ability to triumph over adversity. During the latter part of her life, which was dogged by illness, Cookson gave large sums of money to charity, and much of what is left of her fortune will also go to charitable causes. (→ June 28)

JASPER, WEDNESDAY 10
Race-hate murder in Texas town

Lawrence Brewer, Shawn Berry, and John King – former convicts with alleged Ku Klux Klan connections – were today charged with the murder of disabled black man James Byrd. The three men are said to have chained Mr Byrd to the back of a pick-up truck and dragged him to his death along a dirt-track road. His head was found a mile away from his mangled torso. Law enforcement officers and relatives were agreed that the crime was racially motivated, but both called for calm.

LONDON, SUNDAY 7
Stones abort tour over tax bill

The Rolling Stones today cancelled the British leg of their current world tour, claiming that new Budget tax regulations would make them subject to a tax bill of £12 million.

The four concerts were due to be held during the summer but have been postponed until the next tax year. Mick Jagger apologized to Stones fans but said the group had no option but to call off the concerts.

London, Monday 8. Fans hold a candlelit vigil as a memorial service for Linda McCartney is held at St Martin-in-the-Fields. Among the many celebrities joining Sir Paul McCartney at the service were the other surviving former Beatles, Ringo Starr and George Harrison.

PC used CS gas on pensioner

PC Andrew Taylor was cleared of assault by Luton Crown Court today. He had twice fired his CS spray at Kenneth Whitaker, a 67-year-old pensioner who had parked on double yellow lines. The Police Complaints Authority also cleared Taylor, but admonished an inspector and two sergeants after Mr Whitaker had been held in a police station for nine hours. Civil rights groups expressed disquiet at the ruling.

Montreal, Sunday 7. Michael Schumacher leaps for joy on the podium after winning the Canadian Grand Prix in his first victory of 1998. (→ June 28)

Japanese economy hits the rocks

Financial markets across the globe slumped when it was announced today that Japan's economy was officially in recession. The economy had shrunk by an annual rate of over five per cent, while a falling yen was again put under pressure on foreign exchanges. The loss of confidence in the Japanese economy – the second largest in the world – led to fears that China might also be sucked into Asia's economic turmoil.

Brave Scotland beaten by Brazil

Scottish midfielder John Collins celebrates his 38th-minute goal, which brought Scotland back on level terms with Brazil.

The sixteenth World Cup kicked off with the long-awaited match between world champions Brazil and perennial underdogs Scotland. Unlike many opening matches, the game was a relatively lively affair. Although Brazil scored in the fourth minute with a goal from Cesar Sampaio, Scotland fought back resolutely and drew level with a penalty from John Collins.

While Brazil possessed the superior technique, they were unable to dominate a Scottish team whose confidence grew during the second half. After nearly an hour of play Scotland almost took the lead when Kevin Gallacher's shot was cleared off the line by Cafu. The deciding goal also came from Cafu's efforts, when his shot on goal was punched away by Jim Leighton only to rebound into the net off hapless Scottish defender Tommy Boyd.

The carnival atmosphere of the opening game reflected the festivities on Paris's Place de la Concorde last night, when the start of the World Cup was celebrated with giant statues and dancers in exotic costumes. The festivities were marred by violence, however, as youths threw stones and bottles at police. (→ June 15)

Scottish manager Craig Brown revels in the enthusiasm of the Scottish fans.

June

S	M	T	W	T	F	S
	1	2	3	4	5	6
7	8	9	10	11	12	13
14	15	16	17	18	19	20
21	22	23	24	25	26	27
28	29	30				

Copenhagen, 14
Queen Margrethe of Denmark opens Europe's longest suspension bridge, over the Great Belt waterway. The bridge is 1,624m (5,328ft) long.

Salt Lake City, 14
With an 87-86 victory over Utah Jazz, the Chicago Bulls, led by Michael Jordan, win the National Basketball Association title for the third consecutive season.

Britain, 15
The new £2 coin goes into general circulation, although it will not be in widespread use for some months.

London, 15
Hannah Thompson, 25, a talented young violinist who became a drugs "mule" smuggling cocaine into Britain, is sentenced to four years in prison.

Bordeaux, 16
In the World Cup, Scotland draw 1-1 with Norway, thanks to a goal from Craig Burley. (→ June 23)

Britain, 16
"Headline" inflation – the inflation figure that includes mortgage interest payments – rises to 4.2 per cent, the highest level for six years. There are fears that interest rates will rise.

Santa Monica, 17
Jonathan Norman, convicted of stalking Hollywood director Steven Spielberg with the intention of raping him, is sentenced to 25 years in jail.

Cardiff, 17
The Sony record company signs up 12-year-old Welsh soprano Charlotte Church for a five-album contract initially worth an estimated £100,000.

Bristol, 18
James Wisheart and John Roylance, two doctors involved in the treatment of 29 children who died after heart surgery at Bristol Royal Infirmary, are struck off the medical register. A third doctor, Janardan Dhasmana, is banned from operating on children. Health Secretary Frank Dobson announces that a public inquiry will be held into the affair. (→ October 27)

Westminster, 18
The Government disappoints trade unionists by revealing that the new national minimum wage will be set at £3.60 an hour, with an even lower rate of £3.00 an hour for younger workers.

LONDON, SATURDAY 20
Prince lists what he likes – and what he doesn't

On the eve of Prince William's 16th birthday, the Palace has released some private details of his life to the press, including an intriguing list of the young man's likes and dislikes.

Apparently, he likes his school, Eton, action movies, techno music, and fast food. His dislikes include being a pin-up and dealing with female adulation – a shame, given his current status as a teen idol.

MANCHESTER, THURSDAY 18
Louise flies in to a storm

British au pair Louise Woodward returned to Britain from Boston today, after a Massachusetts court upheld her conviction for the manslaughter of baby Matthew Eappen, but confirmed her release.

A popular cause last year, Louise is currently facing harsh attacks in some newspapers. She told a press conference at Manchester airport: "I feel very sorry for the death of baby Matthew, but I had nothing to do with his death." She later went home to Elton, Cheshire. (→ June 22)

Convicted of manslaughter, au pair Louise Woodward arrives back in Britain.

MARSEILLES, MONDAY 15
England win first match as World Cup fever grips the nation

David Batty connects with a Tunisian player's face while attempting a bold overhead kick.

England came to a halt at lunchtime today as people crowded around televisions to watch the national side embark on their quest to win the World Cup, playing lowly Tunisia.

Manager Glenn Hoddle controversially failed to include England's most highly-rated young hopefuls, Michael Owen and David Beckham, in the starting line-up. Owen came on as a late substitute.

In the event, England performed well enough, winning 2-0 through a headed goal from captain Alan Shearer and a spectacular strike by midfielder Paul Scholes. (→ June 16)

LONDON, WEDNESDAY 17
Police chiefs apologize to Lawrences

A senior officer in the Metropolitan Police, Assistant Commissioner Ian Johnston, today apologized to the family of murdered black teenager Stephen Lawrence for the failure to bring his killers to justice. In a statement to the public inquiry being held into the murder, Mr Johnston admitted, "We have let you down".

Speaking on behalf of himself and Commissioner Sir Paul Condon, he said: "I can understand and explain some of what went wrong. I cannot and do not seek to justify it."

Neville Lawrence, Stephen's father, accepted the apology, but added: "We do not forget that Stephen's killers are still free." (→ June 30)

England supporters enter the fray in Marseilles

The French authorities today threatened English football hooligans with mass expulsion after two days of violence on the streets of Marseilles.

The expected trouble started on Sunday in the Old Port area of the city. Drunken English fans fought running battles with French police and opposing supporters. Some 40 people were injured and up to 100 arrests were made. There were further disturbances both during and after the England game against Tunisia the following day.

British politicians were swift to denounce the troublemakers. Sports Minister Tony Banks denounced the hooligans as "drunken, brain-dead louts", but praised the behaviour of "the great majority of decent fans".

Toulouse, the venue for England's next match, is now bracing itself to receive the invading army of England supporters, estimated to number around 20,000. Most have no tickets for the match. A few of those arrested in Marseilles have already been given jail terms or deportation orders. (→ June 18)

An England supporter is taken into custody by French police during the riots in the Mediterranean port city of Marseilles.

Ascot, Tuesday 16, and Lens, Sunday 14. Women catch the summer sporting bug: Jamaica were at the World Cup finals for the first time, attracting fervent support (right), although they lost their first match 3-1 to Croatia. There was also glamour at Ascot (left), but the World Cup was hard to avoid.

Rows about Beckham, beans, and "bovver"

As World Cup fever grows, the British press has focussed its attention on every detail of life at the England training ground at La Baule in Brittany. Major debate has arisen over the fact that baked beans have been cut out of the players' diet in favour of poached fish and broccoli.

More pertinently, from a soccer point of view, midfielder David Beckham yesterday spoke to the press about feeling "devastated" at being left out of England's first World Cup match. "I have not come to terms with it even now," he said.

But obsessing the press and politicians more than any other topic is hooliganism. Prime Minister Tony Blair today urged employers to sack convicted hooligans. He said that the "small minority" of troublemakers had to be "eliminated". (→ June 21)

June

Lens, 21
German football hooligans go on the rampage. The violence leaves one French riot policeman in a coma. (→ July 26)

San Francisco, 21
At the Olympic Club, American golfer Lee Janzen triumphs in the US Open.

Lord's, 21
South Africa's cricketers beat England by 10 wickets in the Second Cornhill Test to go one up in the series. (→ July 27)

London, 22
Louise Woodward is interviewed on *Panorama* about her conviction for manslaughter in the United States.

Fleetwood, 22
Jane Couch, 29, becomes the first woman to be granted a professional licence to box by the British Boxing Board of Control, after a lengthy struggle.

Westminster, 22
The House of Commons votes by a majority of 207 to cut the age of consent for gay sex from 18 to 16. (→ July 22)

Wimbledon, 24
British tennis star Greg Rusedski pulls out of the Wimbledon tournament with an ankle injury. (→ June 29)

London, 24
After supporting New Labour for 18 months, *The Sun* publishes a front-page picture of Tony Blair with the banner headline: "Is this the most dangerous man in Britain?" *The Sun* opposes Labour on European monetary union.

London, 25
The Queen officially opens the new British Library. Sited in St Pancras, the library has cost £511 million to build.

Nottinghamshire, 27
Diane Blood, the widow who won a battle in the Court of Appeal last year for the right to take her dead husband's frozen sperm abroad for fertility treatment, reveals she is pregnant.

DEATHS
June 22. Benny Green, jazz musician and broadcaster, dies of cancer at the Royal Marsden Hospital, Fulham, aged 70.

June 22. Maureen O'Sullivan, Irish-born American actress famous for playing Jane in the 1930s Tarzan movies, mother of Mia Farrow, dies aged 87.

Greenwich, Monday 22. Tony Blair, together with Deputy Prime Minister John Prescott and Peter Mandelson, minister responsible for the Millennium Dome, attend the "topping out" of the Dome – the traditional ceremony to mark the completion of the highest part of a building. (→ October 13)

LYONS, SUNDAY 21
Iran v US – politics takes on football

It was described as "the footballing equivalent of World War III" – Iran v the United States in the World Cup.

The world's media hyped the clash, security was tight, and the atmosphere was charged for the two countries' first sporting contest since the hostage crisis 20 years ago.

President Bill Clinton broadcast a message before kick-off, saying he hoped the match would heal rifts between the nations. But in the end, football held sway over politics. The outcome of the night was that Iran, the superior side, beat the US 2-1, sending the footballing newcomers out of the tournament. (→ June 26)

Iranian supporters showed up in strength to watch their team take on the United States.

CHINA, TUESDAY 24
Feathered find links dinosaurs to today's birds

Two feathered dinosaurs have been discovered in north-east China, giving added support to the theory that birds are descended from dinosaurs.

The creatures have been named *Protarchaeopteryx robusta* – probably the ancestor of the first true bird – and *Caudipteryx zoui*. Slender and turkey-sized, their feathers were probably used for camouflage, display, or insulation rather than flight. But the fact that they had feathers at all provides a link to modern birds.

NORTHERN IRELAND, SATURDAY 27
Ulster elections produce a workable Assembly

The Good Friday peace agreement emerged the shaky victor, alongside David Trimble's Ulster Unionist Party, in the elections for Northern Ireland's assembly this week.

Mr Trimble, who will be named first minister next week, called the result a "clear mandate for the peace agreement". Up to 75 per cent of the votes were for parties in favour of the agreement.

The Ulster Unionists emerged the single largest party with 28 seats. Dissident Unionists who oppose the peace deal needed 30 seats to block Trimble's victory and wreck co-operation with nationalists in the assembly – but fell short with 28.

John Hume's SDLP is the leading nationalist force in the assembly, with 24 seats to Sinn Fein's 18. (→ July 9)

First defeat, then England find winning formula

After a bumpy ride earlier in the week, England's World Cup campaign is back on track. Glenn Hoddle's young team stormed into the second round after a spectacular 2–0 victory over Colombia in Lens last night.

England came to this fixture trailing clouds of anxiety. A last-minute defeat by Romania in Toulouse on Monday night knocked the confidence of the team, and meant they had at least to draw to avoid a humiliating first-round exit from France.

Hoddle, knowing he could hold nothing back, started the two players whom the press and public had been clamouring for: David Beckham and Michael Owen. Both vindicated the huge expectations placed on them, particularly Beckham, who was stunning in the central midfield role.

Darren Anderton scored first in the 20th minute, and Beckham found the goal 10 minutes later with a free kick that curled past Colombia's right-hand goal post.

But England's loss on Monday has still cost them dear. Group leaders Romania have drawn Croatia in the next round, while England take on more fancied opponents – their old enemy Argentina. (→ June 30)

Dejection: Captain Alan Shearer after Romania's 2-1 victory from an injury-time decider.

St Etienne, Tuesday 23. A Scotland fan watches in despair as his team exit the World Cup after losing 3-0 to Morocco. It ends Scotland's dream of reaching the tournament's second round for the first time – but the resilient Tartan Army still partied in St Etienne into the night.

Elation: Beckham proves his worth to Glenn Hoddle with his first international goal.

June

S	M	T	W	T	F	S
	1	2	3	4	5	6
7	8	9	10	11	12	13
14	15	16	17	18	19	20
21	22	23	24	25	26	27
28	29	30				

China, 28
President Bill Clinton, on an official visit to China, criticizes the Communist regime's human rights record in comments that are broadcast live to the Chinese people on television and radio.

Magny-Cours, 28
German driver Michael Schumacher wins the French Grand Prix. His Ferrari colleague, Eddie Irvine, takes second place. Schumacher's victory puts him only six points behind Mika Hakkinen, who has led the drivers' championship since the first race of the season.

London, 28
A girl has a narrow escape when a giant crane near Boston Manor station tips over and crashes into her bedroom.

Newcastle, 28
Less than a month after the death of novelist Catherine Cookson, her husband Tom dies at the age of 87. Friends say he died of a broken heart.

Wimbledon, 29
British tennis star Tim Henman defeats Australian Pat Rafter in four sets to reach the Wimbledon quarter-finals for the third year running. He will face the No. 3 seed Petr Korda. (→ July 3)

London, 30
An ambulance is called to the home of former TV presenter Paula Yates. She is known to have been in a depressed state since the death of her lover, the singer Michael Hutchence, last November, and earlier this year she revealed that she had considered suicide. (→ July 1)

Iraq, 30
An American jet launches a missile attack on an Iraqi radar site after sensors on board the aircraft show the radar as "locked on". It is the first strike against Iraq since autumn 1996.

Buckingham Palace, 30
Details of royal travel expenses are published for the first time. They reveal that the Royal Family spent £17.3 million on travel last year – despite the fact that the Duke of Edinburgh and Princess Margaret use senior citizens' rail passes to buy cheap tickets.

DEATHS
June 30. Galina Brezhneva, daughter of the former Soviet leader Leonid Brezhnev, dies aged 69.

LONDON, MONDAY 29
Rape is "not the worst thing" says feminist

Novelist Fay Weldon, 66, one of the most prominent British feminists, has distressed many of her admirers with controversial remarks about rape.

In an interview published in the *Radio Times*, Weldon argues against defining rape as "some peculiarly awful crime". Basing her view partly on her own experience as a victim of attempted rape, the writer says "rape isn't the worst thing that can happen to a woman if you're safe, alive, and unmarked after the event."

Weldon has often courted controversy. Earlier this year, she criticized women for leading men on and then refusing sex, saying: "Don't ask a man into your bed and then complain that he touches you up!"

Her comments today have been denounced by women's groups, who fear that her remarks might discourage women from reporting rape.

WASHINGTON, D.C., TUESDAY 30
Tripp testifies on Clinton's relations with Monica Lewinsky

Former White House staffer Linda Tripp sets out for the grand jury hearing.

Linda Tripp, the woman who may bring down the Clinton presidency, testified before a grand jury today.

Tripp secretly taped conversations in which Monica Lewinsky spoke of having oral sex with the president.

Rejecting accusations of having betrayed a friend's confidence, Tripp told the press that she had been motivated by "horror at the abuse of power and the emotional anguish Monica has endured". (→ July 28)

LONDON, TUESDAY 30
Violence at Lawrence inquiry as five suspects testify

The appearance of the five men named as suspects in the murder of black teenager Stephen Lawrence has brought turmoil to the public inquiry into the case over the last two days. The men, Neil and Jamie Acourt, Luke Knight, David Norris, and Gary Dobson, have all been charged at various times in connection with the murder, which occurred in Eltham, south London, in 1993. None has been convicted.

Yesterday, as Jamie Acourt began to give evidence, members of the black militant group, Nation of Islam, identically dressed in dark suits and red bow ties, forced their way into the building in the Elephant and Castle where the inquiry is being held. Scuffles with police led to two arrests.

This afternoon, fighting broke out as the five men left the inquiry together. A crowd that had gathered outside jeered and threw objects at them. Some of the protesters broke through a police cordon to confront the men, and kicks and punches were exchanged. After the suspects had driven off, fighting continued between protesters and the police.

The five men issued a statement today in which they vehemently denied any involvement in the killing of Stephen Lawrence. They said that they sympathized with the Lawrence family's tragic loss, but had "no knowledge of this murder".

The inquiry has uncovered major deficiencies in the original police investigation of the murder. The Lawrences allege that police racism is to blame. (→ October 1)

Protesters make their views known to the five suspects as they leave the Lawrence inquiry.

England are out of the World Cup

England striker Michael Owen goes down in the penalty area in spectacular style. Shearer scored from the penalty that resulted.

David Beckham is sent off for retaliation at the start of the second half, reducing England to desperate resistance.

Glenn Hoddle comforts Paul Ince after the match. Ince was one of two players who missed penalties in the shoot-out.

In a match of high drama and passion, an England team reduced to 10 men tonight held the much-fancied Argentinians to a 2-2 draw until the end of extra time, only to lose the resulting shoot-out through missed penalties by Paul Ince and David Batty.

The game opened in extraordinary fashion with two penalties in the first 10 minutes, one for each side. Then 18-year-old Michael Owen lit up the evening with a goal of outstanding quality, racing through the Argentinian defence and curling his shot past goalkeeper Carlos Roa. England seemed on top, but Argentina equalized just before half time.

The turning point of the game came when David Beckham was sent off for a petulant kick at an opponent's leg. From then on, England fought a lion-hearted rearguard action until the penalty shoot-out proved their undoing.

Disappointed coach Glenn Hoddle said: "We could not have asked more from the players. Everything went against us." (→ July 12)

S	M	T	W	T	F	S
			1	2	3	4
5	6	7	8	9	10	11
12	13	14	15	16	17	18
19	20	21	22	23	24	25
26	27	28	29	30	31	

Bournemouth, 1
A religious education teacher, Robert Fraser, is forced to resign from his job after his school discovers that he has been working as a stripper in the evenings.

Northern Ireland, 1
Ulster Unionist Party leader David Trimble is elected first minister of the new Northern Ireland government as the province's assembly meets for the first time. Seamus Mallon of the Social Democratic and Labour Party is elected second minister. (→ July 2)

Roehampton, 1
TV presenter Paula Yates is admitted to a private clinic after an apparent suicide attempt yesterday.

Malibu, 1
Barbra Streisand marries her boyfriend, TV actor James Brolin. The ceremony is held at short notice in an attempt to evade media attention.

London, 2
Former England cricketer Geoffrey Boycott is reinstated in the BBC's Test match commentary team. He was dropped after a French court found he had assaulted a girlfriend, but the conviction has been set aside. (→ October 20)

St Albans, 2
Footballer Vinnie Jones is sentenced to 100 hours' community service and a fine after being found guilty last month of assault and criminal damage.

Northern Ireland, 2
Loyalist extremists burn 10 Catholic churches across Northern Ireland. Prime Minister Tony Blair visits the province and calls for an end to such "acts of barbarism and violence". (→ July 9)

Wimbledon, 3
Tim Henman, the first British player to qualify for a Wimbledon men's singles semi-final in 25 years, loses to Pete Sampras in four sets. (→ July 4)

Wimbledon, 4
Czech Jana Novotna wins the women's singles for the first time, beating France's Nathalie Tauziat. It was Novotna's third appearance in a singles final. (→ July 5)

DEATHS
July 5. Johnny Speight, creator of the 1960s TV series *Till Death Us Do Part*, dies of cancer aged 78.

SUSSEX, THURSDAY 2

Billie-Jo's murderer jailed for life

Sion Jenkins, the foster father of murdered teenager Billie-Jo Jenkins, was sentenced to life imprisonment at Lewes Crown Court today after a jury found him guilty of the killing.

Thirteen-year-old Billie-Jo was beaten to death in the garden of her Hastings home in March 1997. Her foster father was charged after tests on his clothing revealed minute traces of Billie-Jo's blood.

Sion Jenkins appeared to be an upstanding member of the community. He was a deputy-headmaster and a regular churchgoer. But investigations showed that he had faked the qualifications that got him his job, and had a history of violence against his wife and children.

In a statement to the press, Jenkins' estranged wife, Lois, said the loss of Billie-Jo had been "almost too much to bear". She added: "It is a terrible thing to realize that the man with whom you have lived for 14 years, the father of your children, is capable of murdering your child."

Sion Jenkins leaves Lewes Crown Court during his trial for the murder of Billie-Jo.

Hyde Park, Sunday 5. Prince Charles poses with girl group All Saints, who performed today in front of 100,000 fans at the Party In The Park, a concert in aid of the Prince's Trust. Melanie Blatt (on the Prince's left) charmed the crowd by proudly displaying her pregnancy between her top and pants.

50th anniversary of the NHS

Over 1,800 people came together in Westminster Abbey today for a service to honour the 50th anniversary of the National Health Service. Prince Charles represented the Royal Family and Prime Minister Tony Blair made one of the speeches.

The NHS was founded on July 5, 1948. One speaker at the service, Allison John, whose life was saved by liver, heart, and lung transplants, told the congregation: "I was just lucky to be born in an era when the NHS was available and people like me were able to benefit."

Linford Christie wins libel case

Sprinter Linford Christie today won a libel action over allegations of drug-taking made in an article by former convict John McVicar.

The article, published in a satirical magazine, *Spiked*, in 1995, argued that Christie had probably taken anabolic steroids to enhance his performance. Pleased at the verdict, Christie said: "I am living proof that success achieved after hard, natural, drug-free work lasts so much longer and is so much sweeter."

Beckham apologizes to the nation

A repentant David Beckham arrives at Heathrow after England's World Cup defeat.

Formerly hailed as the golden boy of English football, 23-year-old midfielder David Beckham today faces a personal and professional crisis as critics queue up to blame him for England's early exit from the World Cup. Watched by 23 million Britons on television, Beckham was sent off at the start of the second half of the tie against Argentina after petulantly kicking the leg of an opponent.

The general tone of comment was set by manager Glenn Hoddle's post-match interview in which he blamed Beckham's sending off for the defeat. "I am not denying it cost us the game," he said. Former England coach Bobby Robson was more scathing. He said: "David is a silly offender in this match and he is going to regret it for a long, long time."

This prophecy seems certain to be true. On his arrival back in England today, Beckham issued a statement apologizing for being sent off. "I want every England supporter to know how deeply sorry I am," he said. He described it as "without doubt the worst moment of my career". But in an interview with *The Sun*, he queried the referee's decision: "I certainly didn't feel it was a red-card offence," he said.

This evening Beckham is flying to the United States to be with his fiancée, Spice Girl Victoria Adams.

Sampras makes the history books

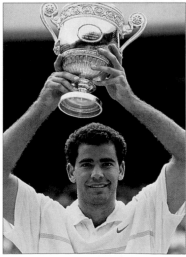

Pete Sampras displays his latest trophy.

Pete Sampras has never been one of the world's most popular tennis players, but his record now proves him one of the greatest ever.

Sampras today beat the Croatian Goran Ivanisevic in five sets to win the Wimbledon men's singles for the fifth time in six years. Bjorn Borg is the only other man to win five championships at Wimbledon since the tournament was thrown open to professionals in 1968.

Sampras did not have an easy victory this year. Ivanisevic took the first set and missed two set points in the second. Apparently on the way out, the Croatian rallied to win a brilliant fourth set, but Sampras was too much for him in the end.

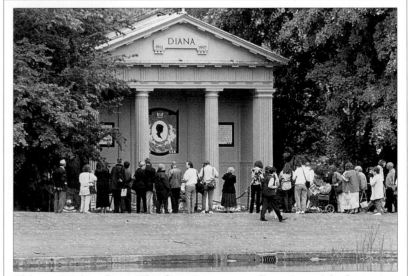

Althorp, Wednesday 1. The first visitors are allowed to visit the grave of Diana, Princess of Wales, at the Spencers' family home. A lakeside Doric temple, now dedicated to Diana, attracted much interest.

S	M	T	W	T	F	S
			1	2	3	4
5	6	7	8	9	10	11
12	13	14	15	16	17	18
19	20	21	22	23	24	25
26	27	28	29	30	31	

London, 6
Caroline Aherne, the actress who plays spoof chat-show host Mrs Merton on television, is admitted to hospital after a suspected drugs overdose.

Milan, 7
Silvio Berlusconi, former Italian prime minister and media mogul, is sentenced to two years and nine months in jail. He was convicted of bribing tax officials.

Lagos, 7
The death of Chief Moshood Abiola, Nigeria's leading opposition politician, sparks riots. Chief Abiola had been in detention since 1993, when the country's military rulers annulled the result of elections he had won.

Northern Ireland, 9
Loyalists storm barricades set up by the police to block the banned Drumcree march. The annual Protestant march traditionally passes through a Catholic area of Portadown. (→ July 14)

Tokyo, 13
The Japanese Prime Minister, Ryutaro Hashimoto, resigns after a humiliating setback in elections to Japan's upper house. Voters judge that he has failed to cure the country's economic malaise as the recession deepens.

Ireland, 13
British cyclist Chris Boardman crashes out of the Tour de France during the second stage, while wearing the coveted leader's yellow jersey. The first two stages of the Tour are taking place in Ireland this year. (→ July 29)

Westminster, 14
Chancellor of the Exchequer Gordon Brown announces a £56 billion increase in public spending over the next three years. About £40 billion of the extra government spending is earmarked for health and education.

St Petersburg, 17
The remains of Russia's last tsar, Nicholas II, and his family, murdered by Bolshevik soldiers 80 years ago, are interred in the Romanov family vault. President Boris Yeltsin says the reburial is an effort "to expiate the sins of our ancestors".

DEATHS
July 6. Roy Rogers, leading Hollywood actor in cowboy movies of the 1940s and 1950s, dies in California aged 86.

Child deaths bring Ulster to its senses

It has taken the tragic deaths of three young boys to rein in a surging wave of Loyalist violence that was threatening to sink the hopes of peace in Northern Ireland.

The three victims, Richard, Mark, and Jason Quinn, lived with their Catholic mother and her Protestant partner on a predominantly Loyalist estate in Ballymoney, Co. Antrim. They were burned to death in a petrol-bomb attack on their home in the early hours of Sunday morning. The boys were aged 11, 10, and 9.

The attack was the culmination of eight days of violence orchestrated by Loyalists opposed to the Good Friday peace agreement. The focus of the Loyalist struggle had become the annual Drumcree march at Portadown, Co. Armagh, banned this year as too provocative. The Loyalist Orange Order vowed last week that the march would go ahead. The police put up barricades to block the marchers and a stand-off developed. Violence flared intermittently at Drumcree and across the province.

Orange Order protesters confront the police across the barricades at the "siege of Drumcree".

The children's deaths, however, made even some of the hardcore Loyalists doubt whether the confrontation should go on. While Dr Ian Paisley called for mass pressure at Drumcree to go on, Robert Coulter, a Unionist member of the Ulster Assembly, said:

"We are burning our children on the altar of our hatred."

As the children are buried today, there are clear signs that Loyalists are drifting away from Drumcree. The cost of violence is at last being seen as too great to bear. (→ August 16)

The coffins of the three Quinn brothers are carried out of the Church of Our Lady and St Patrick, Co. Antrim.

Labour accused of "cronyism"

Revelations about the activities of influential "insiders" close to Tony Blair's inner circle have led Tory leader William Hague to accuse New Labour of "cronyism". Criticism has centred on lobbyist Derek Draper, who is said to have sold access to party leaders such as Peter Mandelson. Blair has rejected accusations of corruption, while agreeing that the rules on lobbying may need tightening.

Paris, Tuesday 7. French soccer star David Ginola has been chosen by the Red Cross to spearhead its campaign against landmines, filling the role once held by Diana, Princess of Wales.

British Grand Prix ends in farce

In torrential rain, German driver Michael Schumacher won the British Grand Prix today, angering Finn Mika Hakkinen, who crossed the line first on the track. The German, it turned out, had already crossed the line in the pits, where, through a stewards' error, he was able to fulfill a 10-second penalty stop after the race had ended. (→ July 26)

Brazil fall apart and France triumph

Brazilian striker Ronaldo walks off dejected at the end of the World Cup final. He almost didn't play after a pre-match breakdown.

The celebrations of the French victory went on throughout the night. It was the first time that France had won the World Cup, and the first time a host nation had won since 1978.

Almost a million people packed the Champs-Elysées tonight to celebrate an unexpected victory for the hosts, France, in the 1998 World Cup. The French trounced a much-fancied Brazilian side 3-0 in the final.

There was a sensation before the match when it seemed that Brazilian striker Ronaldo, billed as the world's greatest footballer, would not play. It appears that the player suffered a seizure earlier in the day and only declared himself fit an hour before the game. His performance was below par, and the whole Brazilian team turned in a lacklustre display.

France owed their victory to star midfielder Zinedine Zidane, who scored twice. The other goal was scored by Emmanuel Petit. French President Jacques Chirac hailed the victory as a sign of national renewal.

July

S	M	T	W	T	F	S
			1	2	3	4
5	6	7	8	9	10	11
12	13	14	15	16	17	18
19	20	21	22	23	24	25
26	27	28	29	30	31	

Papua New Guinea, 19
Thousands are believed dead after a tidal wave sweeps away whole villages on the north-west coast of Papua New Guinea.

Westminster, 22
The House of Lords votes by 290 to 122 to reject a bill that would have lowered the age of consent for homosexual sex from 18 to 16. The House of Commons will now decide whether to re-submit the bill to the Lords. (→ August 5)

California, 22
Anna Murdoch files for divorce from media mogul Rupert Murdoch. A court will decide how much of the Murdoch empire, valued at around $30 billion, she is entitled to.

Spielberg, 26
Mika Hakkinen wins the Austrian Grand Prix, ahead of his McLaren teammate David Coulthard. (→ August 2)

Southampton, 27
The mayor of Southampton, Michael Andrews, and another passenger, Peter Shave, are killed when a flying boat carrying them crashes in the Solent.

Trent Bridge, 27
England's cricketers win the Fourth Test of the series against South Africa by eight wickets. The series is now all-square with one match to play. (→ August 10)

Washington, D.C., 28
Independent prosecutor Kenneth Starr announces that Monica Lewinsky has been granted immunity from prosecution in return for giving a full account of her relations with President Bill Clinton to a grand jury. (→ July 31)

Britain, 30
Olympic silver-medal winner Roger Black resigns as captain of the Great Britain team after not being selected to run in the 400m at the European Championships in Budapest. (→ August 23)

Washington, D.C., 31
President Bill Clinton says he is "looking forward" to testifying to a grand jury about the Monica Lewinsky affair. Meanwhile, the FBI begin examining stains on one of Lewinsky's dresses, said to be the president's semen. (→ August 6)

DEATHS
July 22. Alan Shepherd, the first American to fly in space, dies aged 74.

Harman out in Cabinet shake-up

In a major Cabinet reshuffle today, Prime Minister Tony Blair openly admitted that his much-trumpeted scheme for comprehensive reform of the welfare system was well off target. The minister responsible for the reform programme, Social Security Secretary Harriet Harman, has been sacked, but her deputy, Frank Field, has not been offered her job. Field, a man who has hitherto regarded welfare reform as his life's work, promptly resigned.

Appointing Alistair Darling as the new social security secretary, the prime minister issued a statement on welfare reform, saying: "We want a lot of action." Dissent between Harman and Field is believed to have blocked progress.

Other notable changes in the reshuffle included a first Cabinet post for Peter Mandelson, who becomes secretary for trade and industry.

In general, Tony Blair's closest associates and supporters have been advanced in the reshuffle at the expense of the various friends and allies of the chancellor of the exchequer, Gordon Brown.

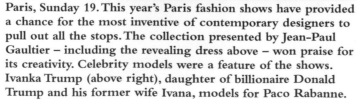

Paris, Sunday 19. This year's Paris fashion shows have provided a chance for the most inventive of contemporary designers to pull out all the stops. The collection presented by Jean-Paul Gaultier – including the revealing dress above – won praise for its creativity. Celebrity models were a feature of the shows. Ivanka Trump (above right), daughter of billionaire Donald Trump and his former wife Ivana, models for Paco Rabanne.

Rose blossoms in the Open

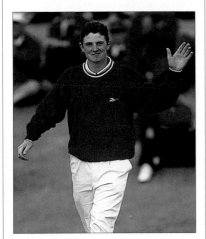

British amateur golfer Justin Rose.

The British Open at Royal Birkdale has been won by American Mark O'Meara, following up his victory in the US Masters last April. But the real star of the occasion was the golfer who tied for fourth place, 17-year-old British amateur Justin Rose. The South-African-born teenager is almost certain to turn professional after a performance that puts him on the verge of world-class status.

Johannesburg, Sunday 19. South African President Nelson Mandela enjoys a joint 80th birthday party and wedding celebration at the side of his new bride, Graca Machel. Singers Michael Jackson, Stevie Wonder, and Nina Simone were among the 2,000 guests present at the televised gala banquet.

Tour de France in chaos over drugs allegations

The Tour de France, the world's top cycling event, has been rocked this year by a drug-taking scandal on an unprecedented scale.

Last week the Festina team was suspended from the race after two of its members admitted using a banned performance-enhancing hormone, erythopoietin (EPO). Since then, police have carried out a series of raids on team hotels, arresting cyclists in the middle of the night and subjecting them to humiliating searches.

Cyclists have reacted by staging sit-down strikes and go-slows. They admit that drug-taking is rife in cycling, but claim that the pressures of the sport make it inevitable.

Today, five teams pulled out of the Tour in protest at police harassment. Laurent Jalabert, France's top cyclist, was among those who withdrew. He said: "Cycling is a family, but it is heading for divorce. The Tour has lost respect for the riders." (→ August 2)

Cyclists on the Tour de France stage a sit-down strike after harassment over drug abuse.

Bentley cleared 45 years too late

On January 28, 1953, 19-year-old Derek Bentley was hanged for the murder of PC Sidney Miles. Today, in the Court of Appeal, the Lord Chief Justice, Lord Bingham, overturned the murder conviction, declaring that the trial judge, Lord Goddard, had denied Bentley "that fair trial which is the birthright of every British citizen".

The killing occurred during a bungled robbery in Croydon in November 1952. PC Miles was shot by Christopher Craig, who was 16 and thus too young to be executed. Bentley was deemed to have urged Craig to carry out the killing by shouting: "Let him have it, Chris."

The execution of Bentley, who had a mental age of 11, caused an outcry at the time. His family are asking today why it took so long for the injustice to be recognized.

August

S	M	T	W	T	F	S
						1
2	3	4	5	6	7	8
9	10	11	12	13	14	15
16	17	18	19	20	21	22
23	24	25	26	27	28	29
30	31					

Paris, 2
Italian cyclist Marco Pantani wins the Tour de France, although his victory is overshadowed by the allegations of drug abuse that have marred the race.

Hockenheim, 2
Mika Hakkinen wins the German Grand Prix to open up a 16-point lead at the top of the drivers' championship table. British driver Damon Hill comes fourth, his best placing this season. (→ August 30)

London, 5
At the Lambeth Conference, Anglican bishops reject homosexual practices as incompatible with the scriptures and call for abstinence from sex outside marriage.

Ireland, 6
Olympic swimmer Michelle Smith is suspended from competition for four years after the sport's governing body decides she doctored a urine sample with alcohol to spoil a drug test. Smith will appeal against the decision.

Devon, 9
More than 100 holidaymakers at Torbay need medical treatment after their feet are slashed by razor-fish shells hidden in the sand on two beaches.

City of London, 11
British Petroleum (BP) announces it is taking over the US oil giant, Amoco, at a cost of £68 billion.

Britain, 13
England football coach Glenn Hoddle faces criticism over comments made in his book *Glenn Hoddle, The 1998 World Cup Story*, currently serialized in *The Sun*. (→ September 3)

Moscow, 13
The Russian stock exchange goes into free fall as American billionaire George Soros describes the state of Russia's financial markets as "terminal". Stock markets in Britain and the United States have also fallen by over 10 per cent in the last month, shaken by the financial crises in Russia and the Far East. (→ August 17)

Britain, 14
An ICM opinion poll for *The Guardian* shows that Prince Charles is more popular than at any time in the last four years.

DEATHS
August 5. Todor Zhivkov, former dictator of communist Bulgaria, dies aged 86.

WASHINGTON, D.C., THURSDAY 6
Lewinsky testifies on White House sex sessions

Monica Lewinsky arrives at a Washington court to give her testimony to the grand jury.

Bill Clinton's presidency today entered its most perilous phase yet as the former White House trainee Monica Lewinsky, 25, testified before a grand jury about her alleged relationship with the president.

Grand jury hearings are secret, but there is little doubt of the story that Lewinsky has to tell. The press is certain she will recount details of frequent oral sex sessions with the president, as revealed last January in taped conversations handed over by her friend Linda Tripp to independent prosecutor Kenneth Starr.

Both Lewinsky and President Clinton have denied under oath that they had an affair. Starr's legal team has negotiated for months to induce Lewinsky to change her testimony, offering her immunity from prosecution for the original perjury.

The president will also have to undergo the humiliation of testifying before the grand jury. If the jurors find that he lied under oath or organized a cover-up, he could face impeachment. (→ August 20)

HAMPSHIRE, SUNDAY 9
Freed mink a threat to local wildlife

Animal rights activists have released thousands of mink from a farm near Ringwood in the New Forest. A massive exercise is under way to recapture these fierce predators as reports flood in of mink attacking local wildlife and pets. A member of the Animal Liberation Front spoke of "liberating" the mink from "concentration camp conditions".

A mink recaptured after a spell on the run.

HEADINGLEY, MONDAY 10
England win a major Test series for the first time in 12 years

England players dance for joy after Darren Gough takes the last South African wicket.

In a cricketing cliffhanger, England won the Fifth Test against South Africa by 23 runs this morning. The victory meant they had won the series 2-1, their first major Test series triumph since 1986-87.

A match of high quality and great drama left South Africa needing 34 to win this morning with two wickets remaining. A crowd of 10,000 watched England pick off the last two batsmen in a tense half-hour.

The England captain, Alec Stewart, said: "We have been through some difficult times. Hopefully this will be the beginning of some good times."

Bombings of US African embassies leave 257 dead

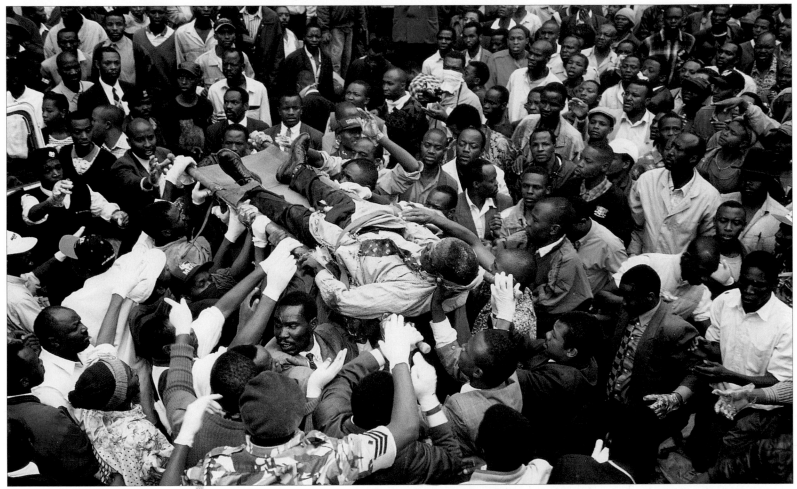

A local victim of the Nairobi bombing is carried away on a stretcher. Most of the dead and injured were innocent Kenyans who happened to be in the area of the blast.

In a murderous double attack today, terrorists bombed the US embassies in Nairobi, Kenya, and Dar-es-Salaam, Tanzania. Both of the attacks occurred at about 10.30 a.m., and no warning was given before the huge car bombs exploded outside the embassies, to devastating effect.

More than 250 people are feared dead in the two bombings, and the injured may number as many as 5,000. Although the United States was clearly the terrorists' target, only 12 Americans are among the dead. Local office workers and passers-by made up the majority of the victims.

More than 90 per cent of the casualties occurred in Nairobi. A four-storey office block behind the US embassy collapsed, trapping many hundreds of people in the rubble. Local emergency services were completely overwhelmed by the scale of the human disaster.

The embassies had clearly been selected by the terrorists as "soft targets". They were not considered high-risk; the Tanzanian embassy in particular had only light security. No one has admitted responsibility for the bombings, but they are believed to be the work of Islamic extremists. Intelligence agencies initially suggest that the most likely culprit is a Saudi businessman turned international terrorist, Osama bin Laden, who is believed to operate from bases in both Afghanistan and Sudan. In an interview in June, he said: "We predict a black day for America."

President Bill Clinton described the bombings in East Africa as "abhorrent" and "inhuman". In a scarcely veiled threat of retaliation, he said: "We will use all the means at our disposal to bring those responsible to justice, no matter what or how long it takes." (→ August 21)

On August 13, President Clinton and Secretary of State Madeleine Albright wait as the coffins of Americans victims of the embassy bombings arrive at Andrews Air Force Base.

August

S	M	T	W	T	F	S
						1
2	3	4	5	6	7	8
9	10	11	12	13	14	15
16	17	18	19	20	21	22
23	24	25	26	27	28	29
30	31					

Wales, 16
Toddler Liam Evans is found unharmed in a remote area of north Wales after a four-day police search. He was near the body of his grandfather, Gwilym Evans, and the wreckage of the car in which they had been travelling.

Moscow, 17
Russian President Boris Yeltsin allows the rouble to devalue, despite recent assurances that its value would be maintained. It falls by about 50 per cent, leading to panic as Russians attempt to change their roubles for dollars (→ August 27).

Pacific Ocean, 17
American millionaire balloonist Steve Fossett is rescued by Australian yachtsman Laurie Piper after he crashlands in the ocean. Fossett had managed to complete 19,000 km (12,000 miles) of a round-the-world balloon attempt.

Walsall, 18
Reports emerge that some parents have withdrawn their children from a Sunday school run by the Bethany Christian Fellowship after teachers there assert that Diana, Princess of Wales, is in Hell. The teachers, Chris Mansfield and Jeffrey Jones, say the Princess led an immoral life and did not repent before her death.

Northern Ireland, 18
The Real IRA, the terrorist splinter group responsible for the Omagh bombing, declares that it is "suspending military operations". (→ September 1)

Yorkshire, 19
Four people with learning difficulties who are on a barge holiday die when their hired narrowboat sinks in a lock on the Leeds-Liverpool canal.

Manchester, 19
GP Harold Shipman is questioned by police over the death of one of his patients, Kathleen Grundy, who had changed her will to make him chief beneficiary. Detectives say that they are also investigating the deaths of 19 other patients of Dr Shipman. (→ September 7)

Britain, 20
It is revealed that Victoria Adams, better known as Posh Spice, and her fiancé, footballer David Beckham, are expecting a baby in six months time. The couple say that they intend to get married after the birth. (→ September 13)

MIDDLE EAST, FRIDAY 21
US retaliation for embassy bombings fires Muslim protests

The Islamic countries of the Middle East were swept by a wave of anti-American demonstrations today after US cruise missiles struck targets in Afghanistan and Sudan.

The United States launched the attacks yesterday evening in retaliation for last week's bombings of embassies in Africa. The target in Afghanistan was a base used by alleged terrorist chief Osama bin Laden. The target in Sudan was described as a chemical weapons plant, although the Sudanese authorities vehemently deny this. Westerners are fleeing Afghanistan, fearing reprisals by the Islamic fundamentalist Taleban government. (→ August 25)

Muslim demonstrators burn the Stars and Stripes in protest over the US retaliatory strikes.

WASHINGTON, D.C., TUESDAY 18
Clinton fights for political survival

Hillary Clinton, wife of President Bill Clinton, stated today that she loved and forgave her husband after his public admission of a relationship with Monica Lewinsky. But it was still uncertain whether the American people would be as forgiving.

Yesterday, President Clinton was humiliatingly obliged to testify to a grand jury about the Lewinsky affair. Answering questions by television link from the White House, he frankly admitted the relationship, although he apparently refused to reveal some precise sexual details.

In the evening, Clinton addressed the nation on television. He told the American people that he had had "a relationship with Monica Lewinsky that was not appropriate". He said: "I misled people, including even my wife. I deeply regret that." But he did not apologize, only accepting that he had made "a lapse of judgement".

Opinion polls today suggest that Clinton still has the backing of the majority of Americans. But with the press and a Republican-dominated Congress against him, his presidency is still at risk. (→ September 4)

Slaughter:

The people of the town of Omagh, County Tyrone, are in shock today after the worst bomb outrage in Northern Ireland since the current Troubles began 30 years ago.

The car bomb exploded at about 3.10 p.m. on Saturday afternoon, the peak shopping time of the week, in Market Street, Omagh's main thoroughfare. It was also the day of the local carnival, so more people were in the town than usual. The atmosphere was relaxed, as it has generally been in the province since the peace process got under way.

According to the police, a telephone warning was received at 2.30 p.m., but it was inaccurate. The warning said the device was located near the courthouse at the top of Market Street. The police cleared this area, but the bomb actually exploded several hundred yards further down the street.

An eyewitness described seeing "a massive explosion, flash, and smoke, debris flying into the air..." The carnage was instant and appalling. Bodies of the dead and injured lay about the devastated street. People ran in all directions, crying and screaming for help.

The medical services at Tyrone County Hospital were almost overwhelmed by the flood of serious casualties. Fire-fighters played a major part in searching the wreckage of half-demolished buildings.

By today, the death toll had risen to 28. More than 200 people have been injured, many gravely. Political leaders were swift in their condemnation of the bombing. Deputy Prime Minister John Prescott, for

One of the Omagh bomb victims is lifted on to a helicopter to be ferried to hospital.

NORTHERN IRELAND, SUNDAY 16

Omagh bomb kills 28 in shopping-street massacre

Flanked by a grim-faced delegation, Deputy Prime Minister John Prescott gestures angrily towards the site of the bombing during a visit to Omagh the day after the terrorist outrage.

example, expressed his "utter contempt for such a cowardly act". The Queen sent her "heartfelt sympathy" to the bereaved.

But the most unexpected and significant response came from Sinn Fein leader Gerry Adams, who called on the people who planted the bomb to "reflect on the enormity of what they have done and stop now". It was the first time that Adams had openly condemned a terrorist outrage by Republicans – formerly he had only expressed "regret" at bombings.

The bombing is believed to be the work of a Republican splinter group calling itself the Real IRA. The group has been responsible for a series of bombings this year, aimed at disrupting the peace process. Both the British and Irish Governments have stated that they intend to introduce tough new measures against terrorism immediately. (→ August 18)

Northern Ireland, Tuesday 18. The coffins of Avril Monaghan, 30, and her 18-month-old daughter, Maura, are carried for burial at St Macartan's Church. The mother and daughter were both killed in the Omagh bombing, along with the baby's 65-year-old grandmother, Mary Grimes.

August

S	M	T	W	T	F	S
						1
2	3	4	5	6	7	8
9	10	11	12	13	14	15
16	17	18	19	20	21	22
23	24	25	26	27	28	29
30	31					

Britain, 25
European soccer administrators reject proposals for a European Super League being put forward by a private company, Media Partners.

London, 25
BBC Wildlife magazine reports that a new breed of mosquito has evolved in the London Underground. The ancestors of the insects were trapped in the Tube when it was built in the 19th century.

Britain, 25
British Airways signs a deal worth an estimated £3 billion for the purchase of a fleet of European Airbus planes. The order is expected to safeguard thousands of jobs in the British aircraft industry.

Libya, 26
Libyan leader Colonel Muammar Gaddafi accepts a deal proposed by the British Government for the two chief suspects in the 1988 Lockerbie bombing to be sent for trial in the Netherlands. Colonel Gaddafi had previously refused to allow the two men, Libyan intelligence agents, to be extradited to Scotland for trial.

Westminster, 27
Former Conservative Prime Minister Baroness Thatcher says that the current Tory leader, William Hague, has no chance of winning the next general election.

Spain, 29
Kenneth Noye, wanted by the British police in connection with the "road-rage" killing of Stephen Cameron two years ago, is arrested in Spain.

London, 31
On the anniversary of the deaths of Diana, Princess of Wales, and Dodi Fayed, Harrod's owner Mohamed Al Fayed says that if the fatal car crash was not an accident, his "Egyptian curse" would not let the killers escape.

Oval, 31
England's cricketers are trounced by Sri Lanka only three weeks after their series victory over South Africa. Sri Lankan spin bowler Muttiah Muralitharan takes 16 wickets in the match as England lose by 10 wickets. (→ September 3)

DEATHS
August 27. Bob Arnold, the actor who played Tom Forrest in the popular radio series *The Archers*, dies aged 87.

BUDAPEST, SUNDAY 23

British athletes triumphant as they sweep to victory at the European championships

Britain's victorious 4x400 metres relay team: Left to right, Mark Hylton, Mark Richardson, Iwan Thomas, and Jamie Baulch.

Britain's athletes rounded off a superb performance in the European championships with three gold medals in the last half hour of the competition this evening – for Jonathan Edwards in the triple jump, Steve Backley in the javelin event, and the 4x400 metres relay team. This late flurry brought the team's overall tally to nine golds, along with four silver and three bronze medals. Great Britain topped the medal table, ahead of Germany and Russia, for the first time in this competition since 1950.

Edwards said afterwards: "I thought after the gallant losers, in the football and with Tim Henman, it's nice to see the athletes come out on top."

CAPE TOWN, TUESDAY 25

Three die in retribution for US missiles

A bomb exploded tonight at the Planet Hollywood restaurant in Cape Town, South Africa, killing three people and injuring more than 25. British tourists are among the victims. The bombing is believed to be a response to American missile strikes on alleged terrorist targets in Afghanistan and Sudan last week – which were in turn retaliation for the bombing of US embassies in Dar-es-Salaam and Nairobi.

A previously unknown organization called Muslims Against Global Oppression has said it carried out today's attack. An anonymous caller told a Cape Town radio station: "We are going to fight fire with fire."

St James' Park, Friday 28. Dutchman Ruud Gullit, appointed manager of Newcastle United in place of Kenny Dalglish, met the Geordie fans today and promised them "really sexy football".

MOSCOW, FRIDAY 28

Yeltsin stumbles as rouble goes into free fall

President Boris Yeltsin tonight made a dramatic appearance on Russian television to scotch rumours that he was about to resign. He told the Russian people: "I am not going anywhere. I am not going to resign. I am going to work."

But most observers believe that Yeltsin has suffered a fatal loss of authority during the last week. Since he sacked Prime Minister Sergei Kiriyenko on Monday, the rouble has collapsed, losing 60 per cent of its value. Viktor Chernomyrdin, appointed to replace Kiriyenko, has little public support. Long-suffering

Russians, queuing outside banks in the hope of salvaging some of their savings, could only reflect bitterly on the state of their country after seven years of free-market reforms.

Meanwhile, stock markets in Europe and North America, which had survived earlier turmoil in Asia relatively unscathed, are plunging as the Russian economic gloom fuels fears of global financial meltdown. The Dow Jones index has dropped over 500 points in two days and the FTSE 100 index stands at 5,249.4, almost 20 per cent down on its peak earlier this summer. (→ September 1)

London, Sunday 30. It was carnival time today in London's Notting Hill district. More than 200,000 people turned up to see the floats and costumes prepared by the local West Indian community.

BELGIUM, SUNDAY 30

A Grand Prix of shocks and crashes ends in British victory

An ecstatic Damon Hill celebrates his first Grand Prix victory of the season.

In torrential rain, the Belgian Grand Prix today provided one of the most memorable Formula One contests of recent years. Britain's Damon Hill scored an unexpected victory as most of the top names failed to finish.

The race began with a spectacular multiple pile-up. After a restart, another crash put World Championship leader Mika Hakkinen out of the race. His nearest rival, Michael Schumacher, seemed sure to win until Hakkinen's McLaren teammate, David Coulthard, ran into the back of the German. A furious Schumacher accused Coulthard of trying to kill him, but stewards ruled the collision was accidental. (→ September 13)

Mika Hakkinen (left) collides with Michael Schumacher shortly after the restart.

WESTMINSTER, TUESDAY 25

MPs recalled to toughen anti-terror laws

The Government announced today that Parliament is to be recalled from its summer recess to approve emergency anti-terrorist legislation.

The new laws are being rushed through in the wake of the Omagh bombing. The chief purpose of the legislation is to crack down on terrorist factions in Northern Ireland, but it will include powers to prosecute terrorists using Britain as a base for outrages abroad. (→ September 1)

BRITAIN, AUGUST 31

Is the memory of Diana fading?

The first anniversary of the death of Diana, Princess of Wales, passed off quietly today, with few echoes of the mass grieving that swept the nation in the wake of the fatal accident.

Prayers were said for the Princess at churches across the country and many flags flew at half-mast. At the gates of Kensington Palace, Diana's admirers lit candles and left cards and flowers. But the small numbers who turned up at this shrine suggested that people had decided to move on.

September

Moscow, 1
President Bill Clinton begins an official visit to Russia, currently gripped by a political and economic crisis. The Russian parliament is refusing to accept President Yeltsin's nominee, Viktor Chernomyrdin, as prime minister. (→ September 10)

Northern Ireland, 1
In a strong statement in support of the peace process, Sinn Fein leader Gerry Adams declares that violence in Northern Ireland must be "a thing of the past, over, done with and gone". (→ September 4)

Westminster, 2
Prime Minister Tony Blair makes it known that he is opposed to a proposal by the ITV companies to ditch *News at Ten*. They want to replace it with news programmes at 6.30 p.m. and 11.00 p.m..

Lord's, 3
England cricket coach David Lloyd is severely reprimanded by the England and Wales Cricket Board after publicly querying the legality of the bowling action of Sri Lankan spinner Muttiah Muralitharan, who took 16 wickets in a Test against England last month.

County Durham, 3
Japanese company Fujitsu announces that it is closing a microchip manufacturing plant opened only seven years ago in Prime Minister Tony Blair's Sedgefield constituency. Some 600 jobs will be lost.

Bisham Abbey, 3
England football coach Glenn Hoddle and defender Tony Adams appear at a joint press conference to scotch rumours that critical comments made by Adams in his book *Addicted* had caused dissension between the two men. (→ September 5)

Bangladesh, 4
The Bangladeshi Government appeals for international aid as floods engulf about a half of the country's land area.

Stockholm, 5
England's campaign to qualify for the football European Championship finals in the year 2000 gets off to a bad start with a 2-1 defeat by Sweden. Midfielder Paul Ince is sent off. (→ October 9)

DEATHS
September 1. Lord Rothermere, the publisher of the *Daily Mail,* the *Mail on Sunday,* and the *Evening Standard,* dies of a heart attack, aged 73.

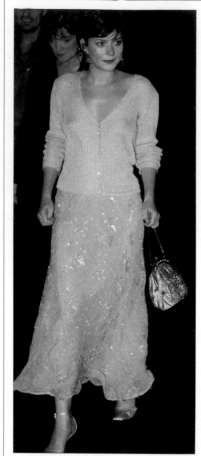

London, Wednesday 2. Former *Brookside* actress Anna Friel attends the opening of the movie *Land Girls*, in which she stars with Rachel Weisz.

Swissair crash in the Atlantic leaves more than 200 dead

Accident investigators are today struggling to understand how a Swissair McDonnell Douglas MD-11 airliner came to crash in St Margaret's Bay off the Atlantic coast of Nova Scotia. All 229 people on board are believed dead. They included eight Britons and at least 10 United Nations officials.

Swissair Flight 111 got into difficulty an hour after leaving New York for Geneva in the early hours of this morning. The pilot, Captain Urs Zimmerman, reported a fire on board. He used the signal "Pan, Pan, Pan", which indicates a crisis that the pilot believes can be coped with, rather than "Mayday", the signal used in desperate circumstances. He first turned the aircraft back to make an emergency landing at Boston, Massachusetts, but then changed course again, heading for a nearer airport at Halifax, Nova Scotia.

Passengers were told to don their life jackets and Captain Zimmerman brought the aircraft lower, beginning to jettison fuel into the ocean in preparation for landing. Sixteen minutes after the original emergency signal, however, the aircraft disappeared from radar screens.

Wreckage from Swissair Flight 111 scattered over St Margaret's Bay.

Fishermen from the village of Peggy's Cove were joined by local emergency services and Canadian naval vessels in searching the scene of the crash for survivors, but none were found. The aircraft had broken into thousands of pieces, posing a problem for investigators. (→ September 6)

Princes appeal for an end to grieving

On the day that Prince Harry joined his brother William at Eton, the two boys have issued an appeal for an end to public grieving over the death of their mother, Diana, Princess of Wales.

In a statement read out to the press by a member of the royal press office, the two princes said they believed that their mother "would want people now to move on".

They said they had been "comforted enormously" by the public sympathy and support they had received in the year since their mother's fatal accident. But they felt that the time had come for her to be "allowed to rest in peace".

Thirteen-year-old Prince Harry takes his place among the pupils at Eton College.

Clinton visits Ireland and says "sorry" at last

President Clinton is greeted by an enthusiastic crowd in Limerick, but back in the United States his reputation is increasingly under attack.

President Bill Clinton must have hoped to leave his domestic political woes behind him on his current three-day visit to Northern Ireland and the Irish Republic. But the Monica Lewinsky affair has continued to dog his footsteps.

The Clinton trip began on Thursday with Bill and Hillary visiting bomb-torn Omagh with Tony and Cherie Blair. This was followed by an inspiring address to an open-air peace rally in Armagh. Clinton then moved on to the Republic, where he was mobbed by friendly crowds. He plans to end his trip with a round of golf at the famous Ballybunion course tomorrow.

But back in the United States, Clinton has meanwhile been coming under increasing pressure to make a more forthright apology for his behaviour in the Lewinsky affair. Faced with fresh denunciations of his "immorality", he was forced once more to comment on the case in Dublin today. Pressed by reporters, Clinton said he was "very sorry" for his relationship with Lewinsky. It was the furthest he had yet gone in eating humble pie, but the mood of American opinion suggests it is still far from enough. (➤ September 10)

Free Viagra "would bankrupt the NHS"

The Government has made it clear that the "wonder drug" Viagra, about to be licensed for sale in Britain, is not going to be made freely available on the National Health Service.

Viagra is claimed to cure impotence, a condition thought to afflict one man in 10. In the United States, where Viagra is already available, doctors are writing around 25,000 prescriptions a day for the drug. The Government reckons that similar demand in Britain could bankrupt the NHS, and wants to limit the supply of Viagra to people with a real medical problem. The drug will, however, be available through private doctors for around £6 a pill.

White Hart Lane, Saturday 5. Alan Sugar (left), the owner of Tottenham Hotspur football club, has dismissed the club's Swiss manager, Christian Gross (right), after a poor start to the Premiership season. Gross had only managed the troubled London club since November last year. (→ October 1)

September

S	M	T	W	T	F	S
		1	2	3	4	5
6	7	8	9	10	11	12
13	14	15	16	17	18	19
20	21	22	23	24	25	26
27	28	29	30			

Monza, 13
German driver Michael Schumacher wins the Italian Grand Prix at Monza for Ferrari. The victory brings him level with season-long leader Mika Hakkinen in the race for the World Championship title. (→ September 27)

Flushing Meadow, 13
Australian Pat Rafter wins the US Open for the second year in succession. He beats compatriot Mark Philippoussis to become No. 2 in the world rankings.

Blackpool, 14
TUC president John Edmonds calls private sector bosses who award themselves huge pay rises "greedy bastards". Speaking at the first day of the TUC conference in Blackpool, he also criticizes Government economic policy.

London, 18
The Football Association support England manager Glenn Hoddle despite growing disquiet over his handling of the team, the publication of his book, and his promotion of faith healer Eileen Drewery.

Argentina, 20
The Duchess of York's mother, Susan Barrantes, 61, is killed in a car accident near her ranch at Tres Lomas.

The Oval, 21
Leicestershire win the County Cricket Championship with a victory over Surrey, denying second-placed Lancashire a clean sweep of this season's trophies.

Florida, 22
A Florida court frees British nurse Helen Cummings, who confessed to shooting her American husband Tyler over his infidelity. The defence claimed expectant Cummings, 33, was a victim of battered woman's syndrome.

Kuala Lumpur, 22
In a break with protocol, which dictates that she never gives autographs, the Queen signs a football for young Manchester United fans during her visit to Malaysia.

DEATHS
September 13. George Wallace, former governor of Alabama and US presidential candidate, known for his pro-segregation stance in the 1960s, dies aged 79.

September 19. Veteran actress Patricia Hayes, best known for playing comic Cockney characters, dies aged 88.

LONDON, WEDNESDAY 16

Death case fires new police racism accusations

As the inquiry into the Stephen Lawrence murder case continues, the Metropolitan Police are at the centre of another race row, this time over their handling of an investigation into the death of a young black musician.

Michael Menson, 30, was severely burned on the North Circular road in London in February last year. He died of his injuries 16 days later. Police concluded that he had caused his own injuries and did not immediately treat the incident as a crime.

Before he died Menson said that he had been set alight by white youths. Yesterday an inquest found that he had been unlawfully killed. Experts say it is unlikely he inflicted this type of injury on himself.

Little Marlow, Bucks, Sunday 13. Spice Girls singer Scary Spice wed dancer Jimmy Gulzar today. Among the guests, all dressed in white, were Posh Spice Victoria Adams and her footballer fiancé David Beckham, snapped by the paparazzi as they arrived at the event.

OXFORDSHIRE, SUNDAY 20

British hostage pair survive their grim ordeal

Freedom at last: Jon James and Camilla Carr after arriving at RAF Brize Norton. They were held hostage for 443 nights.

After 14 months of captivity in cells in Chechnya, two British charity workers have been set free to return home to their families.

Jon James, 38, and Camilla Carr, 40, had been working for a Quaker-funded children's charity in the Chechen capital of Grozny when they were snatched from their home by six masked gunmen last July.

They were kept without light, but otherwise "treated pretty well, considering", Ms Carr said at a press conference this evening. At 3 a.m. today they were woken and told – not for the first time – they were really going home. However, this time it was true and by 9.20 p.m., they were back on British soil and reunited with their families at RAF Brize Norton in Oxfordshire.

The humiliation of a president

Queen loses her head in new Euro move

Tory MPs reacted with fury yesterday over news that the Queen's head will not appear on Euro banknotes if Britain joins the single currency.

The European Central Bank overruled an earlier decision that space would be left on the notes for "national features" – such as the sovereign's head – saying it would be too inconvenient and would make forgery easier. The new Euro currency will be adopted by 11 countries of the European Union, excluding Britain, in 100 days' time.

Bill Clinton's grand jury testimony is shown on a large screen in Times Square, New York.

It was supposed to be the last nail in Bill Clinton's political coffin. With the president still reeling from the publication of the Starr report into his relationship with White House intern Monica Lewinsky, last week a Republican-dominated committee in the House of Representatives voted to broadcast Clinton's videotaped grand jury testimony about the affair to the American nation.

Advance publicity said his testimony to the grand jury would show an "evasive, angry" man, who swore and at one point stormed out of the room in reaction to some of the questions. Would this tip the scales in favour of Clinton's impeachment?

When the tapes were finally rolled, what the world saw was a composed, if slightly pale and sweaty, Clinton. He showed some annoyance when he challenged whether the detailed sexual questions were legitimate, but there was also charm and amazing verbal fluency during an unprecedented live examination.

Clinton's lowest point came when he struggled to define sexual rela-

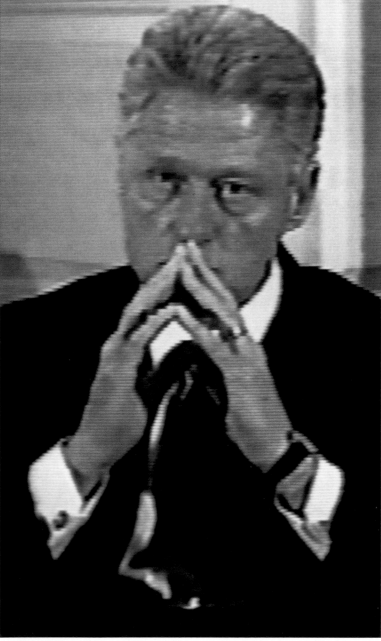

The long-awaited videotape: Americans and the world were promised an "angry", "swearing" presidential performance, but got a controlled and charming Clinton instead.

tions. He admitted to "inappropriate intimate contact" with Lewinsky, but denied any "sexual relations" as he understood them. But his own definition of the term – as being designed to "arouse and gratify" in the "enumerated areas" – was so obscure as to be unintelligible.

When it was all over, the staff in the White House must have breathed a collective sigh of relief. Not only had the president come

across surprisingly well, but no new information had emerged in addition to the details in the Starr report.

Early soundings showed that Clinton's reputation was not severely damaged by the broadcast of his evidence. Although his troubles have by no means vanished, a poll organized for CNN television and *USA Today* showed that support for the president had climbed from 60 per cent to 66 per cent. (→ November 4)

"Fastest woman" Flo-Jo dies at 38

Flo-Jo at the height of her powers, winning at the Seoul Olympics in 1988.

American sprinter Florence Griffith Joyner, who stunned the world with three unexpected Olympic golds in the Seoul games in 1988, has died of an apparent heart attack at the relatively early age of 38.

The flamboyant "Flo-Jo" became the "fastest woman in the world" in 1988, setting 100m and 200m records that have never been beaten. But rumours of drug-taking clouded her career. (→ October 22)

September

Lesotho, 24

Troops from South Africa and Botswana take over and restore calm in Maseru, the capital of the landlocked state of Lesotho, in response to an alleged military coup attempt which sparked off two days of fierce fighting.

Brittany, 25

French swimmer Benoit Lecomte reaches the French coast after swimming 5,950 km (3,716 miles) across the Atlantic from Cape Cod on the east coast of the United States. Lecomte swam for around eight hours a day, resting between times on the deck of a support boat.

Connecticut, 26

British boxer Lennox Lewis successfully defends his WBC heavyweight world title against Croatian Zeljko Mavrovic, winning a hard-fought contest on points.

Hillsborough, 26

Sheffield Wednesday's Italian striker Paolo di Canio pushes referee Paul Alcock to the ground after being shown the red card late in his side's Carling Premiership match against Arsenal. Martin Keown of Arsenal is also sent off. (→ October 23)

Nürburgring, 27

Finnish driver Mika Hakkinen wins the Luxembourg Grand Prix ahead of his German rival Michael Schumacher. Hakkinen now has a four-point lead over Schumacher in the Formula One drivers' championship with one Grand Prix remaining. (→ November 1)

Lord's, 28

The MCC, cricket's leading club, votes to end its 200-year-old ban on women members. This reverses a decision taken seven months ago to uphold the rule restricting membership to men.

Luxembourg, 29

A European Union statistical report shows that 23 per cent of British families are now headed by a lone parent. The European average for single-parent households is only 14 per cent.

DEATHS

September 26. Betty Carter, sophisticated jazz vocalist, dies of cancer aged 69.

September 29. Thomas Bradley, the first black American to be elected mayor of Los Angeles, a post he held from 1973 to 1993, dies aged 80.

Iran agrees to lift Islamic death sentence on author Rushdie

Author Salman Rushdie has been under the protection of Special Branch officers since 1989.

The British Government and author Salmon Rushdie were both hailing a triumph today as Iranian Foreign Minister Kamal Kharrazi publicly renounced the fatwa (Islamic decree) that had forced the novelist to live in hiding for almost a decade.

The fatwa was pronounced by Iran's religious leader, the Ayatollah Khomeini, in 1989 after the publication of Rushdie's *The Satanic Verses*, a novel that many Muslims considered blasphemous. The fatwa called for Rushdie to be killed and offered a £1.2 million reward to his assassins.

In a ground-breaking meeting with British Foreign Secretary Robin Cook, Kharrazi said that Iran had "no intention of taking the life of the author of *The Satanic Verses*, or of encouraging anyone else to do so".

Since the fatwa is a religious injunction, however, it cannot be ended by the foreign minister's declaration. In principle, the death threat against Rushdie remains in force. But the author interpreted the Iranian statement as meaning freedom. "It looks like it's over," he said.

GERMANY, SUNDAY 27
Reign of "king Kohl" is over in Germany

Tonight a new era opened in German politics with the defeat of Chancellor Helmut Kohl, who has led the country for 16 years. In a general election, Kohl's Christian Democrats and their allies, the Christian Social Union, received less than 35 per cent of the votes cast, as against over 41 per cent for their main rivals, the Social Democrats.

The new chancellor will be the Social Democrat leader Gerhard Schröder. He will not command an absolute majority in the German parliament, and will probably have to form a coalition government with the environmental party, the Greens, who took approximately seven per cent of the popular vote.

East Sussex, Saturday 26. In the Sussex village of Peasmarsh, Sir Paul McCartney's daughter Mary marries Alistair Donald, a TV producer. The couple had earlier postponed the wedding because of Linda McCartney's death from breast cancer in April.

Americans flee as hurricane strikes the South

Hurricane Georges left a trail of devastation after passing through the Florida Keys.

Hundreds of thousands of people along the southern coast of the United States are seeking emergency shelter today as Hurricane Georges heads across the Gulf of Mexico towards Mississippi and Louisiana.

The hurricane wreaked havoc in the Dominican Republic last week, killing at least 200 people. Yesterday it struck Florida, causing flooding and tearing roofs off buildings.

The authorities have ordered the evacuation of parts of New Orleans that are threatened by flooding. Some 12,000 people have taken refuge in the city's giant football stadium.

London, Thursday 24. The hottest ticket in town is for David Hare's *The Blue Room* at the Donmar Warehouse theatre, starring Hollywood actress Nicole Kidman and Iain Glen.

Blair calls for "backbone"

In a well-received address to the Labour Party conference today, Prime Minister Tony Blair said there would be no backing down from current Government policies. "Backbone, not backdown, is what Britain needs," he told delegates. He warned of a challenging year ahead, in which there would be attacks from all sides. "Welcome to government," he said.

Arm transplant is a first for medical science

In a pioneering operation, Clint Hallam, an Australian businessman, has had a new forearm and hand transplanted on to his right arm. He had lost his hand and forearm in a chainsaw accident.

The operation was performed at the Edouard Herriot hospital in Lyons, France. The donor was an unnamed French patient who had been pronounced brain-dead.

The medical team that carried out the 13-hour operation was headed by French transplant expert Dr Jean-Michel Dubernard and Australian surgeon Earl Owen. Owen claimed that the operation was "as major a breakthrough as the first heart transplant".

Will Carling split shock

Will Carling photographed with Ali Cockayne and their son Henry.

Former England rugby captain Will Carling has left Ali Cockayne, the mother of his 11-month-old child, for another woman. Confirmed today, the split is an immense blow to the reputation of one of Britain's most admired sports personalities.

Carling, who is divorced, has had a complex private life, including a friendship with Diana, Princess of Wales, but he had seemed to be settling down. A testimonial match on his behalf, scheduled for December, is now almost certain to be cancelled.

Brixton bus driver hits jackpot with first novel

The shortlist of six candidates for this year's Booker Prize, Britain's most prestigious award for fiction, was published today. Along with established authors such as Julian Barnes, Ian McEwan, and Beryl Bainbridge, it includes first-time novelist Magnus Mills.

Mills, 44, is a bus driver operating out of the Brixton garage in south London. Written in his spare time between shifts, his novel *The Restraint of Beasts* is a black comedy that draws on his earlier experience as a casual labourer in the north of England. Mills was apparently paid an advance of around £10,000 for the novel. If he were to win it, the Booker Prize would give him a further £20,000, but Mills is not one of the favourites for the award. (→ October 27)

October

S	M	T	W	T	F	S
				1	2	3
4	5	6	7	8	9	10
11	12	13	14	15	16	17
18	19	20	21	22	23	24
25	26	27	28	29	30	31

New York, 1
The UN Security Council condemns the massacre of ethnic Albanians in Kosovo by Serbs. Nato is preparing for possible air strikes against Serbia. (→ October 12)

White Hart Lane, 1
The former Arsenal and Leeds football manager George Graham moves to White Hart Lane to manage Tottenham Hotspur.

Washington, D.C., 1
Alan Greenspan, head of the US Federal Reserve, claims that the Fed's intervention last week to avoid the LTCM hedge fund going bankrupt had prevented "severe, widespread, and prolonged disruptions" to international financial markets. (→ October 6)

London, 5
The Duchess of York hosts the first of a new chat show series. Broadcast on Sky One, it is called *Sarah – Surviving Life*.

China, 6
Prime Minister Tony Blair and his wife begin an official visit to communist China. Unlike President Clinton, who visited China earlier this year, Blair plays down the issue of human rights.

London, 7
Popular presenter Denise van Outen announces that she is resigning from Channel 4's *The Big Breakfast*.

City of London, 8
The Bank of England's monetary policy committee cuts the base interest rate from 7.5 to 7.25 per cent. The cut is criticized as too timid in the face of the threat of global recession. (→ November 5)

Spain, 8
Twenty French pensioners are drowned when a pleasure boat sinks in Lake Banyoles, near Barcelona.

Wembley, 10
England's footballers are booed off the pitch after a 0-0 draw with Bulgaria in a European Championship qualifying game. In the same competition, Scotland and Northern Ireland scrape wins while Wales record a remarkable 1-2 away win over Denmark. (→ October 14)

DEATHS
October 3. Roddy McDowall, British-born American actor, star of movies including *Lassie Come Home* and *Planet of the Apes*, dies aged 70.

LONDON, THURSDAY 1
Stephen Lawrence's parents reject Met apology

Doreen and Neville Lawrence attend the inquiry into the death of their son, Stephen.

Speaking at the inquiry into the death of black teenager Stephen Lawrence, Sir Paul Condon, Commissioner of the Metropolitan Police, publicly apologized for the police's inability to catch the killers. "I deeply regret we have not brought Stephen's racist murderers to justice," said Sir Paul. "I have set out my personal sorrow and regret at having failed Stephen, his parents, and Londoners. There is a sense of shame in the Met about many aspects of this tragic case."

Sir Paul's apology was, however, rejected by the Lawrence family. Mr Lawrence said: "This is a PR job. The public have no confidence in the police and don't believe a word he is saying." Sir Paul denied that there was institutional racism within the police service, although he acknowledged that the police had not done enough to fight racist crime and harassment.

Shouts of "resign" were heard from the public gallery as Sir Paul Condon left the inquiry, and Mrs Lawrence complained that his "fine words" would not solve racism within the police. Calling on him to resign, she said: "I don't see a way forward for the Metropolitan Police."

MAIDSTONE, THURSDAY 8
Victim Josie relives her ordeal

Through police videos, Josie Russell today described to Maidstone Crown Court how, along with her mother Linda and sister Megan, she was attacked by a hammer-wielding killer close to her home in the Kent village of Chillenden in July 1996. Michael Stone, 38, is on trial for the murders.

Josie was aged nine at the time of the attack. Both her mother and sister were killed by hammer blows to the head. Josie suffered terrible brain damage, but survived. She has only gradually recovered the power of speech. In the videotapes shown to the court, she used model dolls and pictures to help piece together what had happened. The jury were moved by her brave efforts to recall what she called "a horrid day to have to think about". (→ October 23)

Hollywood, Friday 2. Gene Autry, the "singing cowboy", died today aged 91. Autry carved out a successful career in Hollywood, starring in a succession of Westerns that combined rip-roaring action with songs. He insisted that the good guy should never shoot first.

London, Wednesday 7. Judge Richard Gee, accused of a £1 million mortgage fraud, today had proceedings against him dropped after psychiatrists claimed that a trial could pose a serious risk to his life.

BOURNEMOUTH, THURSDAY 8

Tory party still dogged by Europe

In his keynote speech to this year's Conservative Party conference, Tory leader William Hague tried to inspire the party with a new vision, dubbed the "British Way". But the Tories' deep divisions, above all over Europe, remained sadly apparent.

Hague had tried to end the bitter debate on European monetary union by holding a pre-conference poll in the party. A large majority of members voted to back Hague's proposal to reject the single currency until at least the end of the next parliament.

But the referendum totally failed in its aim of stopping party divisions flaring into open conflict. It brought an immediate riposte from former minister Michael Heseltine, who said such a policy would make the Tories unelectable. Tory Euro MP James Moorhouse then announced he was defecting to the Liberal Democrats.

Margaret Thatcher and Edward Heath remain divided over Britain's role in Europe.

Tory divisions were underlined by the presence at the conference of two former prime ministers, Ted Heath and Baroness Thatcher, who have radically opposed views on Europe. It was the Eurosceptic Thatcher who received a standing ovation from the party faithful.

WASHINGTON, D.C., TUESDAY 6

Global turmoil threatens British economy

Brokers on London's international futures exchange watch nervously for the next move on the financial markets.

Addressing the IMF (International Monetary Fund) in Washington, D.C., Chancellor of the Exchequer Gordon Brown today acknowledged that the current economic crises in Asia and other parts of the world would slow down the growth of the British economy.

"With Japan and one quarter of the world in recession," said the chancellor, "every country will be affected by the instability affecting the world economy". He noted that British exports to Asian countries had plummeted by 50 per cent or more since last year.

President Bill Clinton, who also addressed the IMF meeting, said the world economy was facing its worst crisis for 50 years and called for measures to put badly affected countries "back on the path of growth".

The Bank of England's monetary policy committee is now under intense pressure to cut interest rates in Britain as part of an international strategy to counter recession. The FTSE 100 index of leading share prices this week fell to 4,648 points, 25 per cent down from its July peak of 6,179 points. (→ October 8)

October

Basle, 11
In one of the best results of his career, British tennis star Tim Henman beats Andre Agassi in the final of the Swiss Indoor tournament in four sets.

Westminster, 12
Parliament's Committee on Standards in Public Life, chaired by Lord Neill, recommends that spending by political parties in general elections should be limited to £20 million, and that the Government should be obliged to remain neutral in referendum campaigns.

London, 12
Evander Holyfield, holder of the IBF and WBA world heavyweight boxing titles, agrees to fight WBC champion Lennox Lewis next year to establish who is the undisputed king of the ring.

Luxembourg, 14
An unconvincing 0–3 win for England over Luxembourg, the weakest team in their European Championship qualifying group, leads to calls for manager Glenn Hoddle to resign. (→ October 17)

United States, 14
Eric Rudolph, a fugitive on the FBI's "ten most wanted" list, is charged with causing the bomb explosion that rocked the 1996 Atlanta Olympics.

London, 15
Channel 4 and Sky Sports buy the right to broadcast Test matches and other international cricket events in England, in a deal worth £103 million over four years. The BBC expresses its disappointment at losing the rights to home Tests, which it has covered for 60 years.

Britain, 17
England football manager Glenn Hoddle and team captain Alan Shearer both deny reports of a serious row in the dressing room after England's poor display against Luxembourg on Wednesday.

Kosovo, 18
The first members of the 2,000-strong force of international observers arrive in the Serbian province of Kosovo to monitor the withdrawal of troops and the cessation of hostilities.

DEATHS
October 17. Joan Hickson, British actress best known for her TV portrayal of Agatha Christie's spinster sleuth Miss Marple, dies aged 92.

Nobel prize for Ulster peacemakers

The Ulster Unionist leader David Trimble and the Social Democratic and Labour Party leader John Hume have been jointly awarded this year's Nobel peace prize for their roles in the Northern Ireland Good Friday peace agreement.

Hume welcomed the award as "a very powerful statement in support of the peace process", but Trimble was altogether more cautious. Pointing out that peace was not wholly secure, he said "there is an element of prematurity about this".

Republicans were disappointed that Sinn Fein's Gerry Adams was not included in the award. Democratic Unionist Reverend Ian Paisley, on the other hand, dismissed the prize as a farce, "rewarding a deal to satisfy the vile murderers of the IRA".

The winners of this year's Nobel peace prize, David Trimble (left) and John Hume, flank Prime Minister Tony Blair.

Wentworth, Sunday 18. Golfing friends Mark O'Meara (right) and Tiger Woods embrace after an exciting duel in the final of the World Match Play Championship. O'Meara won by one hole to cap a dream year that also brought him the US Masters and British Open titles.

Baroness Jay gives peers their marching orders

Opening a two-day debate on the future of the House of Lords today, Baroness Jay of Paddington declared that the Government intended to press ahead with abolishing the right of hereditary peers to vote in the Upper House. She described the political power of the peerage by right of birth as "glaringly unfair and glaringly outdated".

A royal commission is to be set up to advise on the second stage of Government reform of the Lords, which is intended to create a more modern representative assembly.

Gazza seeks help for alcohol abuse

Paul Gascoigne, one of the most gifted English footballers of recent years, has checked into the Priory Hospital in south-west London to be treated for a drinking problem. There is as yet no indication of how long he might stay.

Paul Merson, another England star who was "dried out", today expressed his support for Gazza. At an emotional press conference, Merson spoke of the agony that Gascoigne would suffer. He said: "It takes a lot of guts to come out and say: 'I've had enough'." (→ November 1)

Britain, Friday 16. British actress Kate Winslet, who starred in the phenomenally successful movie *Titanic*, displays her engagement ring after announcing she is to marry assistant director Jim Threapleton.

Air strike threat recedes as Serbia climbs down

Threatened with Nato air strikes within the next 48 hours, President Milosevic of Serbia today agreed to accept the presence of international observers in war-torn Kosovo. Nato is determined to enforce a UN resolution that calls for an end to fighting in Kosovo, where Serbian forces confront ethnic Albanian guerrillas.

The observers will be ordered to ensure that Serbian troops are withdrawn, that both sides stop offensive action, and above all that there are no more massacres of civilians by Serbian forces. (→ October 18)

Pinochet under arrest in London hospital

General Augusto Pinochet, the military ruler of Chile from 1973 to 1990.

Former Chilean dictator General Augusto Pinochet has been arrested in a London clinic, after Spanish judges applied for his extradition to face charges of murder and torture. Pinochet, who is 82, was woken by police in the early hours of yesterday morning to be told of his arrest.

The general took power in Chile in 1973 in a military coup. At least 3,000 people are believed to have been killed in the crackdown that followed the army takeover, and many thousands more were tortured.

The British Government insists that the proposed extradition is a legal matter and will be decided on its merits. The Chilean Government has protested at the arrest, claiming

Left-wing Chilean demonstrators opposed to Pinochet hold a vigil outside the clinic where the general is being held.

that Pinochet has diplomatic immunity. But Cabinet minister Peter Mandelson said on television that the idea of a brutal dictator claiming immunity "would be pretty gut-wrenching stuff" for most people.

Pinochet's lawyers are preparing to contest the arrest in the courts. Meanwhile, anti-Pinochet protesters, many of whom lost relatives or were themselves tortured under Pinochet's rule, have gathered outside the clinic.

Ironically, Pinochet is an admirer of Britain and gave the British useful assistance during the 1982 Falklands War. He is also on friendly terms with former Tory prime minister Baroness Thatcher. (→ October 21)

October

S	M	T	W	T	F	S
				1	2	3
4	5	6	7	8	9	10
11	12	13	14	15	16	17
18	19	20	21	22	23	24
25	26	27	28	29	30	31

New York, 19
Former Spice Girl Geri Halliwell is appointed as a "goodwill" ambassador for the United Nations. She will be involved in promoting Aids awareness.

Westminster, 19
Home Secretary Jack Straw tells police forces that he will cut their budgets if they fail to meet targets for the recruitment of black and Asian officers.

Northern Ireland, 20
Three members of the Republican extremist Irish National Liberation Army are convicted of the murder of Loyalist Volunteer Force leader Billy Wright in the Maze prison last December.

United States, 20
Former Conservative prime minister Baroness Thatcher tells an American audience that women with illegitimate children should be put "in the hands of a very good religious organization".

France, 20
Cricket commentator Geoffrey Boycott went to court in Grasse to dispute the charge bought against him earlier this year that he beat up former girlfriend Margaret Moore while on holiday in France in 1996. (→ November 10)

London, 21
Baroness Thatcher calls for the release of former Chilean dictator General Augusto Pinochet, currently under arrest in a London clinic. (→ October 28)

Britain, 21
BBC Radio 4 announces that it has lost 500,000 listeners in three months. The station's output was revamped in April, possibly alienating some regular listeners.

California, 22
An autopsy on US sprinter Florence Griffith Joyner ("Flo-Jo") finds that she suffocated during an epileptic fit. The autopsy report denies any link between her death and possible drug abuse.

London, 23
An FA disciplinary hearing bans Sheffield Wednesday's Paolo Di Canio for 11 matches. He pushed a referee to the ground during a game last month.

DEATHS
October 20. Frank Gillard, BBC war correspondent who famously covered the 1944 D-day landings, dies aged 90.

LAS VEGAS, MONDAY 19

Ear-biter Tyson is on his way back to the ring

Sixteen months after he outraged the boxing public by taking a bite out of Evander Holyfield's ear, the former heavyweight world champion Mike Tyson has been given back his licence to box professionally.

Black sports personalities Magic Johnson and Muhammad Ali lent Tyson their support in today's hearing before the Nevada State Athletic Commission. His wife described him as "kind of shy" with "the biggest heart of any man I've met".

Voting 4–1 in favour of allowing Tyson to box again, the commission none the less made it clear that this was "one last chance" for the troubled boxer to make good.

Mike Tyson, alongside his wife Monica, plays up to his fierce reputation during the hearing.

San Diego, Wednesday 21. The New York Yankees celebrate winning this year's baseball World Series with a 4–0 victory over the San Diego Padres. It is the 24th time the Yankees have won the series.

MARYLAND, FRIDAY 23

Hopes for a new Palestinian peace deal

The Middle East peace process was on the road again today after Israel and the Palestinian Authority agreed terms for the next step forward in the region. After nine days of horse-trading, the meeting arranged by the United States at Wye Plantation in Maryland ended with Israel agreeing to withdraw forces from another area of the West Bank, in return for a Palestinian commitment to crack down on terrorist groups.

LONDON, WEDNESDAY 21

Albert Memorial restored to glory

The Queen officially reopened the Albert Memorial this evening, after restoration work that had taken four years and cost over £11 million.

Built in 1867 in memory of Queen Victoria's beloved Prince Consort, the memorial can now be seen in its full glory. The present Queen praised the craftsmen and women who had undertaken the truly monumental task of restoration.

Guilty verdict in Russell case

Josie Russell, the only survivor of the brutal attack in which her mother and sister died, is making a courageous recovery from her injuries.

Michael Stone, a 38-year-old man with a long history of mental disturbance and violent crime, was today found guilty of the murder of Lin Russell and her daughter Megan near Chillenden, Kent, in July 1996. When Josie Russell, the only survivor of the attack, was told of the verdict, she said simply: "Good".

Stone was arrested last year after a psychiatrist suggested to police that he fitted the profile of the killer. He had asked to be admitted to a mental hospital shortly before the murders, but had not been given a bed. There was little evidence against Stone, however, until Damien Daley, who was sharing a cell with him, told the authorities that he had confessed.

The jury found Stone guilty by a majority of 10-2. As the verdict was read out in Maidstone Crown Court, Stone cried: "It wasn't me. I haven't done it." He was given three concurrent life sentences. (→ October 26)

Michael Stone had asked for psychiatric help just days before the Russell killings.

Blue Peter drugs case apology

The BBC today apologized to its viewers for the behaviour of one of its children's TV presenters, Richard Bacon, who has been sacked after admitting using cocaine.

Bacon, aged 22, was a presenter on *Blue Peter*, which is currently celebrating its 40th anniversary. The BBC's head of children's programmes, Lorraine Heggessey, said that Bacon had "let himself and the team on *Blue Peter* down".

Sacked BBC presenter Richard Bacon.

Eddie George on the rack over jobs

Eddie George, the governor of the Bank of England, came under fire from Labour MPs today after he seemed to suggest that job losses in the north-east of England were an acceptable price to pay for beating inflation in the south.

His remarks led to sharp criticism in the House of Commons. Denis MacShane, the Labour MP for Rotherham, called on the governor either to apologize or resign.

George claimed that he had been misinterpreted: He had meant that monetary policy targeted the overall economic situation, not the specific needs of particular regions.

October

Britain, 26

Barry Thompson, a prosecution witness in the Russell murder case, says that his testimony was a lie. The admission casts doubt on the conviction of Michael Stone for the murders last week.

Bristol, 27

As the public inquiry opens into the "Bristol babies" case, grateful patients demonstrate in support of surgeons James Wisheart and Janardan Dhasmana and health trust executive John Roylance, the men disciplined over the babies' deaths.

London, 27

Ian McEwan wins the prestigious Booker Prize for his novel *Amsterdam*. It is the third time he has been shortlisted for the prize, but the first time he has won.

London, 28

The High Court rules that General Augusto Pinochet, arrested pending extradition to Spain, has legal immunity for acts committed when he was ruler of Chile. He will remain under arrest while an appeal is heard by the House of Lords.

Moscow, 28

Russian President Boris Yeltsin retires to a sanatorium for treatment, leaving Prime Minister Yevgeni Primakov in effective control of the troubled country.

Westminster, 29

Trade and Industry Secretary Peter Mandelson refers the proposed BSkyB takeover of Manchester United to the Monopolies and Mergers Commission.

South Africa, 29

The final report of South Africa's Truth and Reconciliation Commission, chaired by Archbishop Desmond Tutu, condemns apartheid as a crime against humanity, but also finds the African National Congress guilty of human rights violations during its anti-apartheid struggle.

Sweden, 30

At least 60 teenagers are killed in a fire at a disco in Gothenburg. Most of the victims are immigrants from the former Yugoslavian province of Macedonia.

DEATHS

October 26. Nicholas Budgen, former Conservative MP and dedicated Eurosceptic, dies aged 60.

October 29. Ted Hughes, Poet Laureate and one of the leading literary figures of recent times, dies of cancer aged 68.

Cape Canaveral, Thursday 29. Aged 77, John Glenn boards the space shuttle *Discovery* to become the oldest man ever to travel in space. Back in 1962, Glenn was the first American to orbit the earth.

BRITAIN, SUNDAY 25

Charles and Camilla reject new "revelations"

The Prince of Wales and Camilla Parker Bowles today issued a joint statement denying that they had had anything to do with a new book containing outspoken criticisms of Diana, Princess of Wales.

The book, called *Charles: Victim or Villain?*, written by journalist Penny Junor, alleges that the Princess was unfaithful to the Prince as early as 1985, and that she made threatening phone calls to Mrs Parker Bowles.

The joint statement said that the book "was not authorized, solicited, or approved" by the Prince or his friend. The Prince felt that the details of his marriage "should be left private and undisturbed". (→ October 28)

BRITAIN, FRIDAY 30

Communities pull together as floodwaters rise

Boating through the streets of Shrewsbury after the River Severn broke its banks, reaching its highest level for 50 years.

After Britain's wettest October since the hurricane year of 1987, large areas of the West Midlands are under water. This follows violent storms in Wales and south-west England last weekend, which caused 12 deaths and extensive flooding.

The rivers now causing the most damage are the Severn and the Wye, both of which have burst their banks. Shrewsbury town centre has been cut off by the rising flood level and Hereford is also badly affected. Hundreds of residents have been

evacuated from their homes. Despite damage estimated to cost over £100 million, however, the police reported that householders, farmers, and shopkeepers in the flood zone were on the whole responding with good humour and communal spirit.

Davies regrets "moment of madness"

Ron Davies was said to be under strain before the incident that led to his resignation.

Former Welsh Secretary Ron Davies today gave his first interview since the mysterious events last Monday night that led to his resignation from the Government. He said it had been "a moment of madness" for which he had paid a heavy price, and which he bitterly regretted. Yet the public was left no wiser as to what exactly he was regretting.

According to Davies, his "serious lapse of judgment" occurred when, feeling stressed after a difficult weekend, he decided to go for a nighttime walk on Clapham Common, near his home in south London. There Davies struck up a conversation with a stranger and went with the man to meet two of his friends in Brixton. They were supposed to have a meal together, but instead Davies was threatened with a knife and relieved of his wallet, his mobile phone, and his car. The following morning he met Prime Minister Tony Blair, recounted the night's events, and resigned on the spot.

Davies was adamant that his nocturnal walk had nothing to do with either sex or drugs, saying that he was involved in "no improper behaviour whatsoever".

Journalists were swift to point out, however, that it was unusual for a politician to resign office merely because he was a victim of a crime, and that Clapham Common is a well-known rendezvous for gay sex. Davies has resolutely refused to discuss his private life. (→ November 2)

Falklands wounds begin to heal

President Menem clasps the hand of the Duke of York, who served in the Falklands.

President Menem of Argentina today laid a wreath at a memorial in St Paul's Cathedral for the servicemen who died in the Falklands War. Menem is the first Argentinian leader to visit Britain since the conflict between the two countries in 1982.

The gesture of reconciliation came during a service attended by Falklands veterans from both sides. They included former Welsh Guardsman Simon Weston, left badly scarred by fire, and the Duke of York, who was a helicopter pilot in the war.

Jenkins proposes electoral shake-up

A commission headed by Lord Jenkins today published a report advocating a thoroughgoing reform of the British voting system.

The aim of the shake-up would be to make the composition of the House of Commons reflect more accurately parties' support among the electorate. To achieve this, Lord Jenkins proposes a complex system, combining the alternative vote – a method for deciding between candidates from party lists by sharing out voters' second choices – with "top-up" MPs directly elected for large constituencies. The Government has broadly welcomed the report.

London, Wednesday 28. During a gala performance at the Lyceum to celebrate his 50th birthday, Prince Charles appears on stage in a sketch with Stephen Fry (left) and Roger Moore. Former Spice Girl Geri Halliwell sang *Happy Birthday* in imitation of Marilyn Monroe's famous serenade to President Kennedy.

S	M	T	W	T	F	S
1	2	3	4	5	6	7
8	9	10	11	12	13	14
15	16	17	18	19	20	21
22	23	24	25	26	27	28
29	30					

Westminster, 2
Former Welsh Secretary Ron Davies, who resigned last week, speaks of the abuse he suffered as a child at the hands of his father, whom he describes as "a very brutal figure". (→ November 8)

Honduras, 4
Laura Arriola, a Honduran woman, is rescued by *HMS Sheffield* in the Caribbean, after being swept 80 km (50 miles) out to sea during Hurricane Mitch. Clinging to pieces of driftwood, she spent a total of six days in the water.

London, 5
The Bank of England finds favour among British industrialists when it cuts the base interest rate by half a point from 7.25 to 6.75 per cent.

Washington, D.C., 6
Leading Republican Newt Gingrich resigns as Speaker of the House of Representatives following the surprise success of the Democrats in the US mid-term elections.

London, 6
Prince Charles rejects the suggestion made in a documentary from London Weekend Television that he would like his mother to abdicate.

South Africa, 9
A revolt by West Indian cricketers, who were refusing to join their team's tour of South Africa because of a pay dispute, is resolved in an agreement brokered by former West Indies captain Courtney Walsh. Brian Lara and Carl Hooper are reinstated as captain and vice-captain.

Ypres, 11
On the 80th anniversary of the end of World War I, a dwindling band of survivors – ranging in age from 97 to 103 – are presented to the Queen, who lays a wreath at the Menin Gate.

Liverpool, 12
Liverpool football club announce that co-manager Roy Evans is leaving the club after 33 years of service. Gérard Houllier will stay as sole manager.

DEATHS
November 3. Bob Kane, cartoonist and creator of Batman, dies aged 83.

November 7. Lord Hunt, mountaineer and leader of the first successful Everest expedition, dies aged 88.

Elections let Clinton off the hook

The nationwide US mid-term elections confounded Republican hopes of inflicting a mortal blow on the Democrats and Bill Clinton's presidency. Although the Republicans maintained their majorities in both houses of Congress, the Democrats lost no seats in the Senate and gained five seats in the House of Representatives. To add to Republican woes, Democratic candidates seized the governorships of New York and California.

President Clinton was jubilant as the results came in. The Republicans had mounted a massive advertising campaign in the run-up to the elections calling on Americans to use their vote to condemn Clinton over the Lewinsky affair. This they have resoundingly failed to do. All political commentators are now agreed that the president is unlikely to face impeachment. (→ November 6)

LONDON, TUESDAY 3
Chancellor remains upbeat on British economy

In his annual pre-budget report, the Chancellor, Gordon Brown, told Parliament that Britain would not be drawn into the growing world recession. He claimed that Britain would recover from the current economic downturn within two years.

Mr Brown's revised forecasts for the coming year were criticized by some economists as being too optimistic, while the Shadow Chancellor, Francis Maude, dismissed them as "fantasy forecasting" based on "Peter Pan economics".

Paris, Sunday 8. British tennis ace Greg Rusedski celebrates after beating the World No. 1 Pete Sampras to win the Paris Indoor open championship. "It was the best victory of my career," said Rusedski.

Formula One season ends in triumph for Flying Finn

Mika Hakkinen wins the Japanese Grand Prix – and the World Championship.

In a closely fought duel between Mika Hakkinen and Michael Schumacher to decide the Formula One World Championship, victory finally went to Hakkinen in the last race of the season in Japan.

In an incident-packed race, which saw Schumacher stall his Ferrari on the grid, Hakkinen drove flawlessly from start to finish. "It was easier than some of the races have been this year," said Hakkinen, "but I was aware this morning of the pressure that was falling on me."

Starting from the back of the grid, Schumacher carved his way through the rest of the field with his customary skill, reaching third place, but a blow-out on lap 31 ended any remote hope of challenging Hakkinen for the lead. As in the previous season, Schumacher and Ferrari had come close to securing victory, but had fallen at the final hurdle.

Davies case leads to orgy of "outing"

The resignation of Ron Davies as Welsh Secretary last month, which led to lurid stories in the press about his alleged homosexuality, has been followed by what some observers regard as a "witchhunt" of members of the Cabinet alleged to be gay.

The rash of revelations began with the "outing" of Trade and Industry Secretary Peter Mandelson on the TV programme *Newsnight*. Then came the forced admission of Agriculture Minister Nick Brown that he was a homosexual. After Downing Street had been contacted by the *News of the World*, claiming that Brown had been engaged in a gay relationship, the minister issued a statement today admitting the affair.

Anger in Downing Street over what they claimed were attempts by the newspaper to entrap Brown reflected a growing unease over the current level of media intrusion into politicians' private lives.

Middlesbrough, Sunday 1. After a spell in a rehabilitation clinic, Paul Gascoigne returns to play for Middlesbrough against Nottingham Forest. The result was a 1-1 draw, with Gascoigne being voted man of the match.

Aid arrives after Hurricane Mitch

Distraught survivors in Nicaragua face an uncertain future in a country devastated by Hurricane Mitch.

The arrival today in Honduras of a US aid delegation, led by the Vice-President's wife Tipper Gore, showed a growing sense of urgency in the international community about the havoc caused by Hurricane Mitch.

Reports suggest that nearly 4,000 Nicaraguans and more than 6,000 Hondurans have been killed by the hurricane, which swept through Central America in late October and early November. But relief workers warn that casualties could rise dramatically as a result of disease and starvation. Prolonged heavy rain has caused much of the damage, sweeping away whole towns and villages in the worst-hit areas.

Promises of aid have come from Europe, Mexico, Canada, and the United States. Nicaragua and Honduras were estimated to have lost half their economic potential, in what Mrs Gore called a tragedy of "biblical proportions". Former US president Jimmy Carter, who was also visiting the area, said full recovery could take at least 15 years. He called for all the region's foreign debts to be cancelled.

Vast areas of low-lying land are submerged by the floods in Honduras.

Facts and figures

Sport

MOTOR RACING

FORMULA ONE DRIVERS' CHAMPIONSHIP

	Driver	Points		Driver	Points
1	Mika Hakkinen (Finland)	100	7	Alexander Wurz (Austria)	17
2	Michael Schumacher (Germany)	86	7=	Heinz-Harald Frentzen (Germany)	17
3	David Coulthard (UK)	56	9	Giancarlo Fisichella (Italy)	16
4	Eddie Irvine (UK)	47	10	Ralf Schumacher (Germany)	14
5	Jacques Villeneuve (Canada)	21	11	Jean Alesi (France)	9
6	Damon Hill (UK)	20	12	Rubens Barrichello (Brazil)	4

HORSE RACING

ENGLISH CLASSIC WINNERS

Vodafone Derby
High-Rise ridden by Olivier Peslier

Vodafone Oaks
Shahtoush ridden by Mick Kinane

Sagitta 1000 Guineas
Cape Verdi ridden by Frankie Dettori

Sagitta 2000 Guineas
King of Kings ridden by Mick Kinane

Pertemps St Leger
Nedawi ridden by John Reid

LEADING NATIONAL HUNT RACE WINNERS

Grand National
Earth Summit ridden by Carl Llewellyn

Cheltenham Gold Cup
Cool Dawn ridden by Andrew Thornton

Champion Hurdle
Istabraq ridden by Charlie Thorn

GOLF

WINNERS OF MAJOR TOURNAMENTS

Major	Venue	Winner
British Open	Royal Birkdale	Mark O'Meara (USA)
US Open	Olympic Club	Lee Janzen (USA)
US Masters	Augusta National	Mark O'Meara (USA)
US PGA	Sahalee Country Club	Vijay Singh (Fiji)

LEADING MONEY WINNERS OF 1998

USA

1	David Duval (USA)	$2,591,031
2	Vijay Singh (Fiji)	$2,238,998
3	Jim Furyk (USA)	$2,054,334
4	Tiger Woods (USA)	$1,841,117
5	Hal Sutton (USA)	$1,838,740

Europe

1	Colin Montgomerie (Scot.)	£933,077
2	Darren Clarke (N. Ireland)	£902,867
3	Lee Westwood (England)	£814,386
4	Miguel Jimenez (Spain)	£518,820
5	Patrik Sjoland (Sweden)	£500,136

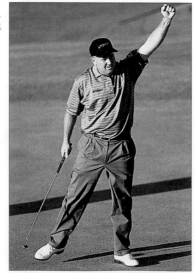

Mark O'Meara celebrates winning the US Masters at Augusta National, the first of his two Major triumphs in the 1998 season.

TENNIS

GRAND SLAM SINGLES WINNERS

Wimbledon
Pete Sampras (USA)
Jana Novotna (Czech)

French Open
Carlos Moya (Spain)
Arantxa Sanchez Vicario (Spain)

US Open
Pat Rafter (Australia)
Lindsay Davenport (USA)

Australian Open
Petr Korda (Czech)
Martina Hingis (Switzerland)

CRICKET

WEST INDIES V ENGLAND TEST SERIES

Test	Venue	Result
1st Test	Kingston	Drawn (match abandoned)
2nd Test	Port of Spain	West Indies won by 3 wickets
3rd Test	Port of Spain	England won by 3 wickets
4th Test	Georgetown	West Indies won by 242 runs
5th Test	Barbados	Drawn
6th Test	Antigua	West Indies won by an innings and 52 runs

West Indies won the series 3–1.

ENGLAND V SOUTH AFRICA TEST SERIES

Test	Venue	Result
1st Test	Edgbaston	Drawn
2nd Test	Lord's	South Africa won by 10 wickets
3rd Test	Old Trafford	Drawn
4th Test	Trent Bridge	England won by 8 wickets
5th Test	Headingley	England won by 23 runs

England won the series 2–1.

ENGLAND V SRI LANKA TEST

Sri Lanka beat England by 10 wickets at the Oval

MAJOR COUNTY TROPHIES

County Championship

Champions	Leicestershire
Runners-up	Lancashire

AXA League

Winners	Lancashire

Benson & Hedges Cup

Final	Essex beat Leicestershire

NatWest Bank Trophy

Final	Lancashire beat Derbyshire

RUGBY

RUGBY LEAGUE

Competition	Winner
Silk Cut Challenge Cup	Sheffield Eagles
JJB Super League	Wigan Warriors

RUGBY UNION

Competition	Winner
Allied Dunbar Premiership	Newcastle
Tetley's Bitter Cup	Saracens

SNOOKER

WINNERS OF MAJOR TOURNAMENTS IN 1997–98

Tournament	Winner
Embassy World Professional Championship	John Higgins (Scotland)
Benson & Hedges Masters	Mark Williams (Wales)
Liverpool Victoria UK Championship	Ronnie O'Sullivan (England)
British Open	John Higgins (Scotland)

SOCCER

FA CARLING PREMIERSHIP 1997-98

		P	W	D	L	F	A	Pts
1	Arsenal	38	23	9	6	68	33	78
2	Manchester United	38	23	8	7	73	26	77
3	Liverpool	38	18	11	9	68	42	65
4	Chelsea	38	20	3	15	71	43	63
5	Leeds United	38	17	8	13	57	46	59
6	Blackburn Rovers	38	16	10	12	57	52	58
7	Aston Villa	38	17	6	15	49	48	57
8	West Ham United	38	16	8	14	56	57	56
9	Derby County	38	16	7	15	52	49	55
10	Leicester City	38	13	14	11	51	41	53
11	Coventry City	38	12	16	10	46	44	52
12	Southampton	38	14	6	18	50	55	48
13	Newcastle United	38	11	11	16	35	44	44
14	Tottenham Hotspur	38	11	11	16	44	56	44
15	Wimbledon	38	10	14	14	34	46	44
16	Sheffield Wednesday	38	12	8	18	52	67	44
17	Everton	38	9	13	16	41	56	40
18	Bolton	38	9	13	16	41	61	40
19	Barnsley	38	10	5	23	37	82	35
20	Crystal Palace	38	8	9	21	37	71	33

Relegated: Bolton, Barnsley, Crystal Palace.

NATIONWIDE LEAGUE

	DIVISION 1	DIVISION 2	DIVISION 3
Champions	Nottingham Forest	Watford	Notts County
Runners-up	Middlesbrough	Bristol City	Macclesfield Town
Also promoted	Charlton Athletic	Grimsby Town	Lincoln City
			Colchester United
Relegated	Manchester City	Brentford	Doncaster Rovers
	Stoke City	Plymouth Argyll	
	Reading	Carlisle United	
		Southend United	

BELL'S SCOTTISH LEAGUE PREMIER DIVISION 1997-98

		P	W	D	L	F	A	Pts
1	Celtic	36	22	8	6	64	24	74
2	Rangers	36	21	9	6	76	38	72
3	Hearts	36	19	10	7	70	46	67
4	Kilmarnock	36	13	11	12	40	52	50
5	St Johnstone	36	13	9	14	38	42	48
6	Aberdeen	36	9	12	15	39	53	39
7	Dundee United	36	8	13	15	43	51	37
8	Dunfermline Athletic	36	8	13	15	43	68	37
9	Motherwell	36	9	7	20	46	64	34
10	Hibernian	36	6	12	18	38	59	30

Hibernian relegated.

OTHER SCOTTISH LEAGUE DIVISIONS

	DIVISION 1	DIVISION 2	DIVISION 3
Champions	Dundee	Stranraer	Alloa
Runners-up	Falkirk	Clydebank	Arbroath
Relegated	Partick Thistle	Stenhousemuir	
	Stirling	Brechin	

MAJOR CUP FINALS IN ENGLAND

FA Cup (sponsored by Littlewoods)
Arsenal 2 Newcastle United 0

Coca-Cola Cup
Chelsea 2 Middlesbrough 0
(after extra time)

MAJOR CUP FINALS IN SCOTLAND

Tennents Scottish Cup
Hearts 2 Rangers 1

Coca-Cola Cup
Celtic 3 Dundee United 0

Scottish League Challenge Cup
Falkirk 1 Queen of the South 0

WORLD CUP FINALS 1998

GROUP A

	P	W	D	L	F	A	Pts
Brazil	3	2	0	1	6	3	6
Norway	3	1	2	0	5	4	5
Morocco	3	1	1	1	5	5	4
Scotland	3	0	1	2	2	6	1

GROUP B

	P	W	D	L	F	A	Pts
Italy	3	2	1	0	7	3	7
Chile	3	0	3	0	4	4	3
Austria	3	0	2	1	3	4	2
Cameroon	3	0	2	1	2	5	2

GROUP C

	P	W	D	L	F	A	Pts
France	3	3	0	0	9	1	9
Denmark	3	1	1	1	3	3	4
South Africa	3	0	2	1	3	6	2
Saudi Arabia	3	0	1	2	2	7	1

GROUP D

	P	W	D	L	F	A	Pts
Nigeria	3	2	0	1	5	5	6
Paraguay	3	1	2	0	3	1	5
Spain	3	1	1	1	8	4	4
Bulgaria	3	0	1	2	1	7	1

GROUP E

	P	W	D	L	F	A	Pts
Netherlands	3	1	2	0	7	2	5
Mexico	3	1	2	0	7	5	5
Belgium	3	0	3	0	3	3	3
South Korea	3	0	1	2	2	9	1

GROUP F

	P	W	D	L	F	A	Pts
Germany	3	2	1	0	6	2	7
Yugoslavia	3	2	1	0	4	2	7
Iran	3	1	0	2	2	4	3
USA	3	0	0	3	1	5	0

GROUP G

	P	W	D	L	F	A	Pts
Romania	3	2	1	0	4	2	7
England	3	2	0	1	5	2	6
Colombia	3	1	0	2	1	3	3
Tunisia	3	0	1	2	1	4	1

GROUP H

	P	W	D	L	F	A	Pts
Argentina	3	3	0	0	7	0	9
Croatia	3	2	0	1	4	2	6
Jamaica	3	1	0	2	3	9	3
Japan	3	0	0	3	1	4	0

SECOND ROUND

Romania	0	Croatia	1
Argentina	2	England	2

(Argentina win 4-3 on penalties)

Germany	2	Mexico	1
Holland	2	Yugoslavia	1
France	1	Paraguay	0
Nigeria	1	Denmark	4
Italy	1	Norway	0
Brazil	4	Chile	1

QUARTER FINALS

Holland	2	Argentina	1
Germany	0	Croatia	3
Italy	0	France	0

(France win 4-3 on penalties)

Brazil	3	Denmark	2

SEMI-FINALS

France	2	Croatia	1
Brazil	1	Holland	1

(Brazil win 4-2 on penalties)

THIRD PLACE PLAY-OFF

Holland	1	Croatia	2

FINAL

Brazil	0	France	3

England captain Alan Shearer fights an aerial duel with the Colombian defence during his side's 2-0 victory in Group G.

Awards

NOBEL PRIZE

Literature
Jose Saramago (Portugal)

Peace
John Hume (UK)
David Trimble (UK)

Physiology or Medicine
Professor Robert F. Furchgott (USA)
Professor Louis J. Ignarro (USA)
Professor Ferid Murad (USA)

Chemistry
Professor Walter Kohn (USA)
Professor John A. Pople (UK)

Physics
Professor Robert B. Laughlin (USA)
Professor Horst L. Störmer (Germany)
Professor Daniel C. Tsui (USA)

Economic Sciences
Professor Amartya Sen (India)

ACADEMY AWARDS ("OSCARS")

Best Picture
Titanic

Best Director
James Cameron for *Titanic*

Best Actress
Helen Hunt for *As Good As It Gets*

Best Actor
Jack Nicholson for *As Good As It Gets*

Best Supporting Actress
Kim Basinger for *LA Confidential*

Best Supporting Actor
Robin Williams for *Good Will Hunting*

Best Original Musical Score
Anne Dudley for *The Full Monty*

Best Foreign-language Film
Character (Netherlands)

Best Cinematography
Russell Carpenter for *Titanic*

Best Original Screenplay
Ben Affleck and Matt Damon for *Good Will Hunting*

Best Adapted Screenplay
Brian Helgeland and Curtis Hanson for *LA Confidential*

Best Art Direction
Peter Lamont for *Titanic*

Best Original Song
My Heart Will Go On from *Titanic* – music James Horner, lyrics Will Jennings

Best Sound Effects Editing
Titanic

Best Costume
Titanic

Best Film Editing
Titanic

Best Visual Effects
Titanic

CANNES INTERNATIONAL FILM FESTIVAL

Palme d'Or
Eternity and a Day directed by Theo Angelopoulos (Greece)

Grand Jury Prize
La Vita e Bella directed by Roberto Benigni (Italy)

Best Director
John Boorman for *The General* (Ireland)

Best Screenplay
Hal Hartley for *Henry Fool* (US)

Best Actor
Peter Mullan for *My Name Is Joe* (UK)

Best Actress
Elodie Bouchez and Natacha Regnier in *La Vie Rêvée des Anges* (France)

Special Jury Prize (shared)
La Classe de Neige directed by Claude Miller (France)
Festen directed by Thomas Vinterberg (Denmark)

BAFTA AWARDS

FILM AWARDS

Academy Fellowship
Sean Connery

Best Film
The Full Monty

Best Actress
Dame Judi Dench in *Mrs Brown*

Best Actor
Robert Carlyle in *The Full Monty*

Best Supporting Actor
Tom Wilkinson in *The Full Monty*

Best Supporting Actress
Sigourney Weaver in *The Ice Maiden*

Best Original Screenplay
Gary Oldman for *Nil By Mouth*

Best Special Effects
The Fifth Element

Best Director (David Lean Award)
Baz Luhrmann for *William Shakespeare's Romeo and Juliet*

Outstanding British Contribution to Cinema (Michael Balcon Award)
Michael Roberts

Outstanding British Film (Alexander Korda Award)
Nil By Mouth

TELEVISION AWARDS

Best Single Drama
No Child of Mine

Best Drama Series
Jonathan Creek

Best Drama Serial
Holding On

Best Light Entertainment Performance
Paul Whitehouse in *The Fast Show*

Best Light Entertainment
The Fast Show

Best Comedy Performance
Steve Coogan in *I'm Alan Partridge*

Best Actress
Daniela Nardini in *This Life*

Best Actor
Simon Russell-Beale in *A Dance to the Music of Time*

INTERACTIVE MEDIA AWARDS

Tim Berners-Lee Award
Peter Kindersley

BRIT AWARDS

Best British Male Solo Artist
Finley Quaye

Best British Female Solo Artist
Shola Ama

Best British Group
The Verve

Best British Producer
Chris Potter

Best Video by a British Artist
All Saints, *Never Ever*

Best Album by a British Artist
The Verve, *Urban Hymns*

Best British Newcomer
Stereophonics

Best British Dance Act
The Prodigy

Best British Single
All Saints, *Never Ever*

Best International Male Solo Artist
Jon Bon Jovi

Best International Female Solo Artist
Bjork

Best International Group
U2

Best Soundtrack/Cast Recording
The Full Monty

Outstanding Contribution
Fleetwood Mac

THE BOOKER PRIZE

Winner
Ian McEwan, *Amsterdam*

Shortlist
Beryl Bainbridge, *Master Georgie*
Julian Barnes, *England, England*
Martin Booth, *The Industry of Souls*
Patrick McCabe, *Breakfast on Pluto*
Magnus Mills, *The Restraint of Beasts*

Finley Quaye was honoured as Best British Male Solo Artist at the Brit Awards.

OLIVIER THEATRE AWARDS

Best Actress in a Play
Zoë Wanamaker in *Electra*

Best Actor in a Play
Ian Holm in *King Lear*

Best Director
Richard Eyre for *King Lear*

Best New Play
Closer by Patrick Marber

Best New Dance Production
Mark Morris Dance Group and English National Opera for *L'Allegro, Il Penseroso, ed Il Moderato*

Best Actress in a Musical
Ute Lemper in *Chicago*

Best Actor in a Musical
Philip Quast in *The Fix*

Best Performance in a Supporting Role
Sarah Woodward in *Tom & Clem*

Best New Opera Production
The Royal Opera for *Paul Bunyan*

Best New Musical
Beauty and the Beast

Politics and Finance

THE CABINET

(After the reshuffle of July 27, 1998)

Prime Minister
Tony Blair

Deputy Prime Minister and Transport, Environment, and Regional Secretary
John Prescott

Chancellor of the Exchequer
Gordon Brown

Foreign and Commonwealth Secretary
Robin Cook

Lord Chancellor
The Lord Irvine of Lairg

Home Secretary
Jack Straw

Education and Employment Secretary
David Blunkett

President of the Council and Leader of the House of Commons
Margaret Beckett

Minister for the Cabinet Office and Chancellor of the Duchy of Lancaster
Jack Cunningham

Defence Secretary
George Robertson

Health Secretary
Frank Dobson

Chief Whip
Ann Taylor

Culture, Media, and Sport Secretary
Chris Smith

Scottish Secretary
Donald Dewar

Northern Ireland Secretary
Mo Mowlam

Welsh Secretary
Ron Davies *

International Development Secretary
Clare Short

Social Security Secretary
Alistair Darling

Minister for Agriculture, Fisheries, and Food
Nick Brown

Leader of the Lords and Minister for Women
Baroness Jay of Paddington

Trade and Industry Secretary
Peter Mandelson

Chief Secretary to the Treasury
Stephen Byers

* Ron Davies resigned as Welsh Secretary in October 1998 and was replaced by Alun Michael.

FINANCE

INTEREST RATES

The chart on the right shows the bank base rate from December 1997 to November 1998. The rate was set at 7.25 per cent in November 1997. It is set monthly by the monetary policy committee of the Bank of England.

7.50

7.25   7.25

6.75

D J F M A M J J A S O N

SHARE PRICES

The chart below shows the level of the FTSE 100 Index of the top 100 UK companies between December 1997 and November 1998. The chart to the right shows the level of the Dow Jones Index of the 30 leading US corporations. Both sets of figures reflect the first trading day of each month and were compiled over the same time period.

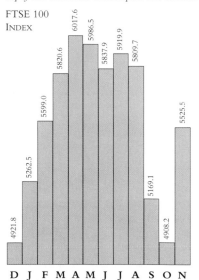

FTSE 100
INDEX

4921.8 5262.5 5599.0 5820.6 6017.6 5986.5 5837.9 5919.9 5809.7 5169.1 4908.2 5525.5

D J F M A M J J A S O N

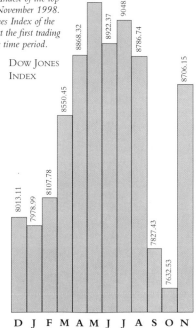

DOW JONES
INDEX

8013.11 7978.99 8107.78 8550.45 8868.32 9147.57 8922.37 9048.67 8786.74 7827.43 7632.53 8706.15

D J F M A M J J A S O N

Obituaries

Actress Joan Hickson died on October 17, 1998.

Acker, Kathy, American novelist, born in April 1944, died November 29, 1997.

Banda, Hastings, former president of Malawi, born May 14, 1906 (official date), died November 25, 1997.

Bono, Sonny, pop singer, born February 16, 1935, died January 5, 1998.

Bremner, Billy, football player and manager, born December 9, 1942, died December 7, 1997.

Bridges, Lloyd, American actor, born January 15, 1913, died March 10, 1998.

Chaplin, Saul, songwriter, born February 19, 1912, died November 16, 1997.

Chisholm, George, OBE, popular jazz musician, born March 29, 1915, died December 6, 1997.

Cookson, Catherine, romantic novelist, born June 20, 1906, died June 11, 1998.

English, Sir David, former editor of the *Daily Mail*, born May 26, 1931, died June 10, 1998.

Gellhorn, Martha, first female war correspondent, born November 8, 1908, died February 16, 1998.

Grappelli, Stephane, jazz musician, born January 16, 1908, died December 1, 1997.

Hayes, Patricia, English comic actress, born December 22, 1909, died September 19, 1998.

Hickson, Joan, Miss Marple in Agatha Christie's detective series, born August 17, 1906, died October 17, 1998.

Huddleston, Archbishop Trevor, anti-apartheid fighter, born June 15, 1913, died April 20, 1998.

Hughes, Ted, appointed Poet Laureate in 1984, born August 17, 1930, died of cancer on October 29, 1998.

Hunt, Lord (Sir John), leader of the first successful ascent of Everest, born June 15, 1913, died November 7, 1998.

Hutchence, Michael, lead singer of Australian group INXS, born January 12, 1960, died November 22, 1997.

Kurosawa, Akira, Japanese film director, born March 23, 1910, died September 6, 1998.

Lawrence, Syd, big-band leader, born June 26, 1923, died May 5, 1998.

McCartney, Linda, campaigner for vegetarianism, born September 24, 1941, died April 17, 1998.

McDowell, Roddy, actor in *Planet of the Apes*, born September 17, 1928, died October 3, 1988.

MacGregor, Sir Ian, former chairman of the National Coal Board, born September 21, 1912, died April 13, 1998.

Morgan, Dermott, comic actor best known for his character Father Ted, born March 2, 1952, died March 1, 1998.

Muir, Frank, humorist, born February 20, 1920, died January 2, 1998.

Passmore, Victor, artist, born December 3, 1908, died January 23, 1998.

Perkins, Carl, member of Californian group The Beach Boys, born April 9, 1932, died January 19, 1998.

Pol Pot, Cambodian dictator and mass murderer, born in January 1925, died April 16, 1998.

Powell, Enoch, politician, born June 16, 1912, died February 13, 1998.

Rogers, Roy, actor best known for his cowboy roles, born November 5, 1911, died July 6, 1998.

Rothermere, Viscount, owner and publisher of the *Daily Mail*, born August 27, 1925, died September 1, 1998.

Shepherd, Alan, astronaut, born November 18, 1923, died July 22, 1998.

Sinatra, Frank, singer, born December 12, 1915, died May 14, 1998.

Speight, Johnny, comic writer, best known for *Till Death Us Do Part*, born June 2, 1920, died July 5, 1998.

Spock, Dr Benjamin, childcare guru, born May 2, 1903, died March 15, 1998.

Tippett, Sir Michael, CBE, composer, born January 2,1903, died January 8, 1998.

Wells, John, satirist, born November 17, 1936, died January 11, 1998.

Wynette, Tammy, country singer, born May 5, 1942, died April 6, 1998.

Zhivkov, Todor, former communist Bulgarian dictator, born September 7, 1911, died August 5, 1998.

Index

Page references in *italics* refer to sidebar entries.

94

Picture credits